Empowering Your Life
with
MASSAGE

Empowering Your Life with MASSAGE

Erica Tismer and Carolyn Flynn

ALPHA

A member of Penguin Group (USA) Inc.

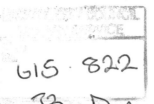

ALPHA BOOKS

Published by the Penguin Group

Penguin Group (USA) Inc., 375 Hudson Street, New York, New York 10014, U.S.A.

Penguin Group (Canada), 10 Alcorn Avenue, Toronto, Ontario, Canada M4V 3B2 (a division of Pearson Penguin Canada Inc.)

Penguin Books Ltd, 80 Strand, London WC2R 0RL, England

Penguin Ireland, 25 St Stephen's Green, Dublin 2, Ireland (a division of Penguin Books Ltd)

Penguin Group (Australia), 250 Camberwell Road, Camberwell, Victoria 3124, Australia (a division of Pearson Australia Group Pty Ltd)

Penguin Books India Pvt Ltd, 11 Community Centre, Panchsheel Park, New Delhi—110 017, India

Penguin Group (NZ), Cnr Airborne and Rosedale Roads, Albany, Auckland, New Zealand (a division of Pearson New Zealand Ltd)

Penguin Books (South Africa) (Pty) Ltd, 24 Sturdee Avenue, Rosebank, Johannesburg 2196, South Africa

Penguin Books Ltd, Registered Offices: 80 Strand, London WC2R 0RL, England

International Standard Book Number: 1-59257-236-7
Library of Congress Catalog Card Number: 2004110006

06   05   04   8   7   6   5   4   3   2   1

Interpretation of the printing code: The rightmost number of the first series of numbers is the year of the book's printing; the rightmost number of the second series of numbers is the number of the book's printing. For example, a printing code of 04-1 shows that the first printing occurred in 2004.

Printed in the United States of America

Note: This publication contains the opinions and ideas of its authors. It is intended to provide helpful and informative material on the subject matter covered. It is sold with the understanding that the authors, book producer, and publisher are not engaged in rendering professional services in the book. If the reader requires personal assistance or advice, a competent professional should be consulted.

The authors, book producer, and publisher specifically disclaim any responsibility for any liability, loss, or risk, personal or otherwise, which is incurred as a consequence, directly or indirectly, of the use and application of any of the contents of this book.

Most Alpha books are available at special quantity discounts for bulk purchases for sales promotions, premiums, fund-raising, or educational use. Special books, or book excerpts, can also be created to fit specific needs.

For details, write: Special Markets, Alpha Books, 375 Hudson Street, New York, NY 10014.

Publisher: Marie Butler-Knight

Product Manager: Phil Kitchel

Senior Managing Editor: Jennifer Chisholm

Senior Acquisitions Editor: Randy Ladenheim-Gil

Book Producer: Lee Ann Chearney/ Amaranth Illuminare

Development Editor: Lynn Northrup

Production Editor: Megan Douglass

Copy Editor: Ross Patty

Illustrator: Hrana Janto

Cover/Book Designer: Bill Thomas

Indexer: Heather McNeil

Layout: Becky Harmon

Proofreading: Mary Hunt

I would like to dedicate this book to the Universal Energy of Love, which is the life blood of All That Is. As such, I dedicate this book to my children: Theron, Mikael, and Sananda, who are my Lifeblood.
—Erica Tismer

To my angels, Lucas and Emerald. You make my heart soar.
—Carolyn Flynn

Contents

Introduction

Touch heals.

In this simple sentence is the kernel of truth that flourished into this book. From the most ancient of times, we have known the healing power of touch. Its power transcends all cultures, all times. Touch is the way a mother expresses love to her child. Touch is the way two lovers express their desire. Touch brings solace to those who grieve.

Touch soothes the soul. It quiets the longing. It bridges the loneliness. It unites two people. Yet it is also a vital way to inform ourselves about the world. Out of curiosity, out of desire to know and experience, we reach out and touch—from picking up a mango from the stall at the roadside grower's market to stroking the soft silk of a hand-painted scarf. Some things, we have to touch to know. In this way, touch can enliven us. It activates all of our senses. It serves to enlighten us.

The healing power of touch is the threshold for *Empowering Your Life with Massage*. Massage is the art of healing touch that transforms. It softens suffering, transmutes pain to calm and inner peace. It substitutes fear, pain, and harshness … with grace. New Age massage goes beyond traditional massage in serving as a vital link between body, mind, and spirit. It draws upon many techniques developed over many cultures to create a wholeness of body, mind, and spirit. In this convergence of wisdom, we find, we can create a deeper awareness—and achieve a quickening of healing and enlightenment.

Do you move through your life with grace? Do you—would you like to—possess within you a deep, abiding, unshakeable peace? Would you like your body's voice to sing in harmony with your mind and spirit? Massage can quell the dissonance within that makes you throb with pain.

In Erica's fingers lie a great wisdom, cultivated by years of training in massage, breath work, and intuition. In her hands reside great compassion, the true essence of healing touch. Our own bodies house this same knowledge of healing, this same compassion and desire for wholeness. Our bodies *know*. This is why they sometimes scream out with pain. This is why they creak and ache and throb. These signals send us to the massage therapist. Massage is the key that unlocks the door to the realm of the body's intuitive knowledge.

New Age massage embraces the sacred traditions of massage across cultures and times. In the pages that follow, we draw upon Native American spirituality, Christianity, Hinduism, Buddhism, Judaism, Sufism, Chinese philosophy, and Toltec wisdom derived from the Aztec tradition. We will blend techniques from classic Swedish massage with Shiatsu and Reiki techniques from Japan, lomi lomi from Hawaii, and polarity work. We will use yoga, chakras, aromatherapy, reflexology, and auras. What all of these hold in common is their strong reliance on intuition as a way of seeking and attaining wisdom. Intuition is the connection that cannot be immediately explained—yet is deeply known. It's the voice we don't always heed in our world of rationalism and intellectualism—the voice that speaks a higher truth. We will use massage to cultivate your ability to hear your body's voice, to know your truest and brightest thoughts and emotions, to open yourself up to an abiding connection to the Divine.

In the weeks after Erica and Carolyn completed this book, each felt a profound loss. Each confessed to feeling something vital was missing. During that time, as Carolyn listened to Erica's soothing voice leading readers through massage exercises, a vital connection was made. Erica was giver, Carolyn receiver. Erica was the woman in the throes of childbirth, Carolyn the midwife. Yet though Carolyn was the receiver: She was giving back to Erica in simply allowing the manuscript to happen, to unfold. Had there been no receiver, there would be no giving. Erica gave *more* because someone was waiting to hear. "When the teacher is ready, the student will appear," is the saying from Buddhist wisdom. And so, we welcome you.

It is our hope that this book will empower you—not just inform you about massage, but point the way for you to use your innate knowledge of healing touch to imbue your life with fulfillment and contentment. Empowerment spills over into every aspect of your life—at work, at home, in partnership, in family, in community. It transforms your relationships with your lover, your mother, your father, your children, your money, your pets, your mind, your sexuality, your Creator. Empowerment is asking the question, "What do I already know to be the truth?" Empowerment is believing you can get there.

Acknowledgments

Writing this book has been an incredible experience. It has highlighted for me, in every moment, where I am now and how I got here—truly a humbling and at the same time, exalting experience. I acknowledge all those teachers along the way; my parents, who told me I could accomplish anything; my dear friend and husband, O. D. Merrick, who has demonstrated to me how to overcome fear of writing; and my first teacher of holistic healing, Robert Stevens, for his intense desire "to know" and his willingness to challenge me to that end.

—Erica Tismer

First, I must acknowledge Erica, whose gentle wisdom and wise touch have expanded my world. For my determination and my love of writing, I must acknowledge my father; for my focus and discipline, I must acknowledge my mother. Both told me I could do anything I set my mind to accomplish. I would be remiss if I didn't acknowledge that my children's father, Myron Saldyt, and his brother, Yuri, are the ones who connected me with Erica. Myron and I continue to teach and heal each other, as we were brought together to do.

I'd also like to thank book producer Lee Ann Chearney of Amaranth Illuminare for picking up on the magic of Erica's touch when I referred to her in *The Intuitive Arts on Health*—and for being the one to push me harder and cheer me on. I'd also like to thank writer extraordinaire Lisa Lenard-Cook, who connected me with Lee Ann. Every writer needs a cadre of supporters, and I'd like to thank my cherished writing group friends: Roma Arellano, Anne Stirling, Nell Burrus, Rose Moore, Judy Anderson, and Teresa Phillips. I extend many thanks to the editors at Alpha, particularly Randy Ladenheim-Gil, Lynn Northrup, and Ross Patty, who made sure the text read perfectly.

—Carolyn Flynn

Trademarks

All terms mentioned in this book that are known to be or are suspected of being trademarks or service marks have been appropriately capitalized. Alpha Books and Penguin Group (USA) Inc. cannot attest to the accuracy of this information. Use of a term in this book should not be regarded as affecting the validity of any trademark or service mark.

Part One

Knowing Your Body Intuitively

We have organized this book in four parts, each representing the deepening wisdom that New Age massage can bring, each representing the planes in which we perceive the world—the physical, the mental, the emotional, and the spiritual. It is said that we first receive information on the spiritual level; if we don't know how to process it, it moves to the mental level. If we don't process it there and integrate the information into our lives, it moves to the emotional level. If we don't address it there, it sinks into the level of the body. There, it gets our attention by becoming what we know as pain. So much of the truth that we receive lies submerged in the pain of the body.

Our first exploration through massage is to unlock the pain of the body. The physical plane represents the first peeling back of the layers that mask the truth. So the journey is about reconnecting with our intuition. And so we begin by tapping into the innate wisdom of the ages that is stored in our bodies, our minds, and our spirits.

Chapter 1

Know How Your Body Feels

From the moment of birth, we have a task: Flesh and spirit must befriend one another. At the first breath of life, we have emerged as a body, and if we are lucky, we have 80-some-odd years for that body to carry around a spirit. This initial union of the spirit with the fragility of the flesh, with all of its pleasures and pains, is the birthing place for this book, *Empowering Your Life with Massage*.

It is at this union of the flesh, the mind, and the spirit that massage plays its role in empowering your life. We believe massage is one of the best ways to connect the mind and spirit to the body. And we believe massage can reveal the body's mysteries and show the way to knowing the mind and spirit.

Why is the union of these three—a body to mind and spirit—so vital to our experience of joy and peace in our lives? A body not connected to the spirit is a body that carries around a general sense of dis-ease. Something is not right. Something is missing. We are not content. We are on the treadmill of life, just trying to keep up with all of our obligations. We are silently asking ourselves, "Is this all there is?"

Yet on the other hand, we were meant to be here, to enjoy life in all of its fullest. We cannot spend all of our time as a hermit in a cave in meditation of the Divine; a lifelong spiritual retreat to the mountains is a luxury. We must make a living, do the laundry, wash the dishes, catch that flight, attend that meeting, return that call, tuck the children into bed, visit mom or grandmom. Our task is to bring the enlightenment of spirit to that life. It illuminates everything we do.

The poignancy of being human is beautifully captured in *Wings of Desire*, a movie by Wim Wenders set in war-scarred Berlin before the fall of the Berlin Wall. Remade in America and set in Los Angeles as *City of Angels*, it stars Meg Ryan and Nicolas Cage. In both versions angels who are watching benevolently over the city long for the pure and simple pleasure and pain of being human, of loving and longing. Sure, it would be nice to be an angel, but what this movie shows is how nice is it to be *human*—to cry, to love, to know joy, to know pleasure, to take risks, to know pain.

With our frenetic lives, it may seem amusing that angels could actually envy our humanity, while we are yearning for the "peace that passeth understanding." How can we find that peace when the muscle in the back of our necks is throbbing in pain, when an ache spreads across our lower back, when a twinge of pain surges through our wrists? We yearn for calmness, for moments of tranquility when we remember our true purpose here. We yearn to experience our lives as we envision them, to experience them fully. We yearn to be comfortable in our own skins, to know ourselves and love ourselves for our true essence.

Massage Is Your Path to Your Self

In this Information Age of data and rationalism, we are trained to hand over our authority to experts. These are authorities outside of ourselves who are specially trained at a university—someone with a law degree who can tell us what the rules are; someone with a medical degree who can tell us the diagnosis with "just a few tests." This transference of responsibility serves to blunt our intuition, to shut out what we already know. We train ourselves to turn somewhere, anywhere else but inside ourselves for the answers. This is how we lose our power.

True empowerment comes from a unity of body, mind, and spirit, a serenity that puts at rest the deep unease we know.

This is not a book just about massage, nor is it another book about handing over your power to yet another expert—the massage therapist. This is a book that will empower *you* to know how you can use massage in your life as a tool. Through this new tool in your life, you will be able to manifest the love, joy, family, community, creativity, health, and abundance you crave. Many other books have been written about massage. But this book will point you in the direction of true, deep, and abiding empowerment, and it will show you how to use massage to get there.

Why do we believe massage is the path? Because the body holds all the tales we would not tell ourselves. The body knows. The body holds our mysteries, the secrets of the ages, the magnificence of our humanity and our divinity.

In this book, we will guide you in using massage to retrain yourself to reclaim your power, so that you may breathe life into the truth of who you are.

Journey to Healing

In Sanskrit, mandala means "healing circle." The circle of the mandala represents, for us, the wholeness of body, mind, and spirit. It can be thought of as a map by which we experience the transformation of our mere mortal minds into the enlightenment of spirit. The journey is from the outer wheel of the circle to the center.

Mandalas can take many forms, and they transcend many cultures, though most of us are familiar with them as a tool used in Tibetan Buddhism. What is common to each is that each object in the journey to the center has a significance, representing a guiding principle or attained wisdom. Throughout this book, we encourage you to begin an Empowerment Journal you will use, much like a mandala, to record your journey from the outside in, to the heart of who you are, and want to become, with massage as your path. In the artwork you will see throughout the book, beautifully rendered by artist Hrana Janto, you will sometimes see the sacred circle used as a visual metaphor to evoke the symbolic journey of self-discovery through massage.

Map of the Heart

One important tool to use as you move through this book is the Empowerment Journal. This will allow you to discover and record your progress as you open yourself to the possibilities that massage can have in your life to manifest the contentedness you seek. For some, it may be helpful to choose a beautifully bound book that symbolizes your intent. For others, a simple spiral-bound or loose-leaf notebook will do.

Throughout this book, look for "Map of the Heart" sidebars to cue you to turn to your Empowerment Journal. It will help you explore your thoughts and know your mind. Consider this the map of your heart. But let yourself open to the process of self-discovery, and don't be limited by our cues. This journal is for you.

Meet Erica and Carolyn

For Erica, the title "massage therapist" doesn't quite fit the bill. It's only a piece of who she is and what she does. She graduated from the New Mexico School of Natural Therapeutics in Albuquerque, New Mexico. But she describes what she practices as the art of healing. Massage is just the way in to that healing. Massage is her gift.

One thing abundantly clear to Carolyn when she first came to Erica several years ago was Erica's high level of intuition. Erica's fingers *knew*. Erica receives a lot of information not just about the muscles and tissue of a person's body, but about that person's mind and spirit, about that person's essence. She comes to a massage with a deep intuitive knowing, a reverence for the true essence of each person. She sees with other eyes, a vision that goes beyond the form of the person in front of her. When she meets someone, she sees who he is now, who he used to be, what he can become. When she touches someone, she can feel that person's joy and sorrow.

Carolyn is a journalist and fiction writer, an editor of a women's magazine and author of other books on New Age health. She is a single mother with many demands. She has been through many changes from the day she first walked into Erica's office. She walked in the door a single woman with a heartfelt desire to create marriage and family and to discover the truest expression of her creativity and her vitality as a woman. Erica has watched her transform from that single woman to married woman to divorced woman, from maid to mother, from a not-very-grounded intellectual trying to gain awareness of her artistic spirit, to unleash her creativity, to a woman who is in her power.

Many people come to Erica not just seeking relaxation or relief for sore muscles but for a journey. They are all ages. They come from all walks of life. They are men. They are women. They come as intellectuals; they come as athletes. They come worried about money or worried about their relationships. They come, perhaps like you, for self-knowing. They come for a new understanding about themselves.

In the Comfort Zone

Massage at its simplest is about comfort. What a difference it makes to have someone rub our shoulders after a hard day. The touch of another can smooth out those stiff, cranky muscles that have stored up tension throughout the day. It's that feeling of "aaaaaaahhhh," the feeling of contentment; we have settled in to where we need to be.

Our cultural attitudes about touch steer us away from the healing touch. American culture is dominated by a strain of Western-thought rationalism and intellectualism, and these times are dominated by technology. We are pushed to stay in the logical world, where there are rules that make sense. Ideas and thoughts dominate our daily lives and quite literally fill up the air, with the Internet. Imagine, for a moment, all the transactions and conversations that fill up cyberspace in the average day on this planet. This is what takes up space in our psyches, leaving very little space for touch, for feeling and for intuiting.

More and more, we interact with others through these barriers—text messaging on our cell phones and e-mail on our computer screens. In the twenty-first century, much of our interaction with other humans takes place through a screen—the computer, the television, and so on.

No wonder it's so refreshing when we experience something tactile. Perhaps there is something to how fashionable velvet has become in recent years. Velvet used to be only for evening wear, but now it's become acceptable in daytime business. Velvet appears in all seasons, not just the holidays. We think it's because in today's world, we spend so much time experiencing life through a screen, that we yearn simply to know what something feels like.

It's ironic that in today's world of e-mail, voice mail, text messaging, instant messaging and so on, there are countless ways to "get in touch" with someone. Despite that, it's actually still somewhat difficult to connect. We spend a lot of time playing phone tag. Slow down for a minute and think about those words, "I just wanted to get in touch with you." Is that what the explosion of communication technology is really all about, we wonder? *Do we just want to be touched?*

The Magic of Touch: Touchstones

Sprinkled throughout this book, you will encounter touchstones. These exercises will serve to remind you how to recapture your sense of touch.

Touch will be vital to your experience of this book. After all, we can't just think about massage. We expect you to experience it. It's a little like believing there is a Divine Being but never actually seeking to know Him/Her. You can't really know the empowering effect of massage unless you touch and are touched.

For this exercise and many others in this book, you will want to recruit a partner. Neither one of you needs to be an expert in massage. The only requirement is that you come to each exercise with a clarity of intention. Erica often says that her utopian world would be one in which there would be no need for massage therapists, that one by one, we would each come to a healing intent, to be shared with another. It is that intent to heal, the compassion and unconditional positive regard, that is central to how another person experiences massage. In other words, it's not about technique.

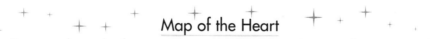

Map of the Heart

Because this is the first exercise, you will want to discuss a few issues with your partner. Think about your energy. Think about whether you are open to giving—and receiving. This is a time for honesty. First you must trust yourself, that you can be honest with yourself. Take a few moments to write in your Empowerment Journal to clarify your attitudes about receiving and giving. Then you must commit to speaking about that with your partner. Over time, there must be a balance between giving and receiving.

To get ready for a massage, you will want to get set up. You can try these exercises with the receiver on the floor on a pillow or mat, but it will be easier to learn proper technique if the receiver lies on a massage table. Because the massage table is ideal for experiencing massage, the exercises in this book are written from that perspective. Contact a local massage school or check local classifieds to find out about buying a sec-ondhand massage table. Folding tables that massage therapists use for house calls or health fairs are a particularly good choice because they are easy to store and are more readily available.

You will also want to gather pillows, towels, and massage oil. Make sure you eliminate distractions such as the phone. You will not want to do the exercises on either an empty stomach or a full one, and you will want to drink plenty of water before, during, and after a massage.

For this exercise, you will be the giver, and your partner will lie on her back. You will sit at her head. Together, close your eyes and take in deep breaths. Breathe out fully, pushing the old breath out. Take two more deep breaths. Let the quiet of the room settle around you. Cup your hand at the base of your partner's head, known as the occipital ridge, at the juncture of head and neck. Ask her to relax her head, let-ting the weight of it sink into your hand. Now place your hand across her forehead, palm down. In this way, the palms are facing each other, cupping, if you will, your partner's head. This completes a circle. Hold this in place for one minute, each deeply breathing.

Say: "Feel the gentleness of the touch of another. Feel the calm. You are not alone. You are being held."

If either one or both of you feels a sigh of contentment, the sense that this just feels right, you've got the magic of touch.

Now, switch places.

A New Place

Have you ever noticed that when you have a massage, after a certain point when you are relaxed and have let go of some of the day's tensions, you have a great insight? Your mind may have been working away at a problem all day—or even for months—but then suddenly you see it in a whole new way.

We believe this happens because massage allows you to anchor into a new place in your body—a healing, safe place. It's not just about physical relief from day-to-day pain and stress. We think not being anchored to this safe place inside is why so many of us spend much of our time outside of the awareness of spirit, in a reactive mode when everything external is creating our thoughts and actions. No wonder we feel so powerless: We feel like we are at the mercy of what other people are doing and saying to us. We spend too many moments of our lives not in awareness that the universe is designed for our own joy, that peace is what is intended for us, that it merely awaits us.

Once anchored in a safe place in your body, you can become aware of that spirit, of the goodness that awaits you. Without that anchor, it's scary to think about how beautiful you are inside, about how magnificent is the joy that is your inheritance. Massage can create an immense abode of safety.

Empowerment Exercise: Creating the Anchor

Throughout this book, you will see empowerment exercises. These will signal you to exercises that will activate your understanding of the role of massage. In other words, roll up your sleeves.

The goal of this exercise, which is to be done with a partner, is to breathe into a safe place within you.

Lie on your back. With your partner's hands on your abdomen, take three deep breaths, one by one, very slowly. Exhale before the first inhale. Push out the breath from where it is now. Push it out as deeply as you can. Let go. Fill yourself up with breath, filling up at the abdomen, pushing your partner's hand up. You should feel a real sense of expansion. Then let it drop down. Let the breath fall gently. Breathe out deeper, deeper, deeper until you just can't breathe out anymore. Do this two more times, drawing breath in to the abdomen. You should feel as if there is a vessel inside you, an expansive place that is very, very safe. As you relax and begin to breathe normally, you will have a sense of receptivity.

We have just created a safe place within you that will serve as an anchor during massage. If at any time doing exercises in this book or during a massage, you start to feel fear, return to this technique.

Now, switch places.

New Massage Traditions

So you can see that it is about more than technique—the way another lays his hands on your body. Swedish massage, which is the massage technique that we are most familiar with, focuses on different types of strokes—the way the massage therapist manipulates the muscles and tissue of the body. Its emphasis is more on stimulation than relaxation, though the decidedly American twist on it involves relaxation. The strokes are very vigorous. The aim is to stir things up in order to purify. Still, Swedish massage can open up some of the same avenues that New Age massage can because there is magic inherent in touch.

Swedish massage became popular in the nineteenth century in the West. It was developed by Per Henrik (1776–1839), a Swedish physiologist and fencing master. You may already be familiar with some of the basic movements of Swedish massage. Henrik gave them French words: stroking (*effleurage*), kneading (*petrissage*), circular pressures (*frictions*), and percussion (*tapotement*).

New Age massage can best be described as massage techniques that honor the wholeness of the body, mind, and spirit. By incorporating the traditions of massage from many cultures, new age massage provides a larger array of techniques that open the recipient to a higher awareness.

We will explore the wisdom of *qigong*, the ancient Chinese art of cultivating and enriching your life force for improved physical, mental, and spiritual health. Out of that came Taoism, Buddhism, and Confucianism, not to mention traditional Chinese medicine with its use of acupuncture, herbs, and more. From ancient China a train of thought developed Shiatsu massage, a Japanese technique that emphasizes acupressure—pressure at points along the energy meridians. We will explore the wisdom of ayurveda, quite literally "science of life" in Sanskrit, and draw upon the discipline of yoga and energies of the chakras. From Hawaii, we have a style of massage called lomi lomi that uses rhythm and movement. From Native American spirituality, we will apply healing techniques that reflect the reverence for the earth and all life forms, as well as the importance of ritual.

We Are Interconnected

Everything that affects us spiritually affects us emotionally or physically. Everything that affects us physically affects us spiritually. It is all interconnected. In new age massage, we believe that energy rolls through us in a progression—from spiritual to mental to emotional to physical. If we do not process it on the spiritual level, it moves to the mind so our minds can perceive it. If we still don't get it, it comes up in our emotions. When we fail to examine our emotions, it manifests itself physically.

Ray of Light: A Mandate to Heal

Sprinkled throughout this book, you will encounter Ray of Light sections. These are anecdotes of illuminating experiences clients have had with Erica that will illustrate the magic of the experience of massage.

James is a 42-year-old African American who had suffered from migraines for most of his adult life. He is a professional with many commitments, but his migraines were so debilitating that once or twice a month he would miss several days of work. By the time he came to Erica, he was taking the maximum dose of his medication with no significant results.

Through a series of five sessions, James had dramatic results. Massage and breath work relieved the headaches after their onset, but during his third session James received information from his higher self. Many memories and images started flickering through his mind and his body. And then he received a mandate. He was directed to make significant changes in his habits.

James told Erica that this intense sense of rightness stayed with him for days and weeks afterward. The massage activated a strong reaction in his body on a deep, feeling level, and he went with it. He did not let other stuff get in his way. It is too easy to let life pile the other stuff right back on, but James did not let it slide. He kept it in the forefront.

From there, James made big changes. He took a hard look at his diet, questioning whether his body really wanted him to be eating the way he had been. Over the next three months, James changed his eating habits, eased off on a strenuous exercise routine, and added regular bodywork. He says he has not had a headache since the fifth session. He now comes in once a month for a tune-up.

> Wisdom is the principal thing;
> Therefore get wisdom. And in all your getting, get understanding.
> —King Solomon, Proverbs 4:7, Holy Bible

Sometimes we wait until our bodies are breaking down or crying out in pain before we pay attention. It's like the universe has to club us over the head. Our goal is to teach you through massage to recognize when the universe is trying to get your attention—*before* your body is screaming at you.

Radio Waves

In the city of Albuquerque, a cluster of radio towers sits on the Sandia Mountains. The lights glitter all night in a sparkling red cloud above the city. You can see them from just about any vantage point in the city. Our bodies are like these radio towers, collecting signals constantly. If you want to know the answer, you already have collected the information you need. The only problem is, there is often a lot of static. We believe massage can cut through the static so that you can hear the one true voice of yourself and the Divine.

Another of the traditions we will draw upon in this book is that of Toltec wisdom, a system of beliefs and practices made known in the 1960s and 1970s by Carlos Castaneda and more recently by don Miguel Ruiz (in his book *The Four Agreements*) and Thuen Mares. A Toltec is a man or woman of knowledge. Toltecs believe that personal growth requires action. The path begins with stalking, or tracking, self-knowledge, and the approach is often compared to that of a warrior.

The student of self-knowledge learns how to stalk himself much the way a hunter stalks his prey or a special law enforcement agent profiles a criminal. A way of describing it is to say "aligning energies." You must know how the animal behaves, how the criminal thinks, in order to encounter it. So it's more than collecting data; you must experience what the animal experiences in order to know how it thinks.

Stalking Yourself

In this exercise, the animal you are stalking is yourself. Get to know yourself and how you work. It may seem obvious to you, but when you consider slowing down to take the time to look at the components of your life, you will realize how unique you are.

Map of the Heart

As you do the exercise for stalking self-knowledge, consider again the mandala, and its sister, the labyrinth, such as the famous labyrinth at Chartres cathedral in France. Sit in meditation on each of the stalking exercise sections. As you go deeper into the labyrinth to find your most true self, release any tension in your wrists, ankles, or neck by stretching them slowly in a circling motion. Keep your Empowerment Journal close by to record your thoughts and impressions after you emerge from your period of meditation.

Your habitat: community and family

Who is your family? Make a list of all the roles you play in life. Man/woman, mother/father, son/daughter, wife/husband. Which of these roles are most prominent in your life? To which are you giving the most energy? To which would you like to give more energy? Which are depleting you?

_____

_____

_____

Describe your community. Is it easy to make friends and break into new social circles? Do you have people outside of your immediate family you can rely on? Is your community like-minded? Is it very diverse? Are there many resources? Are there many people like you in your community, or do you feel somewhat excluded because you are different?

_____

_____

_____

Your trail

What are the circles you move in? Who are your primary influences? Do you associate with people who are your socioeconomic peers? Your intellectual peers? Your spiritual peers? Think about who influences these areas of your life.

_____

_____

_____

Would you describe your life as fast-paced or slow-paced? Would you describe your world as big or small?

_____

_____

_____

How do you play? What do you do for enjoyment?

_____

_____

_____

Your sustenance

How would you describe your diet? Do you practice moderation? Too many sweets? Too much salt? Too much caffeine? Too much alcohol? Do you drink enough water? Do you take vitamins and other supplements?

_____

_____

_____

How do you exercise? Would you consider yourself active or sedentary? Do you incorporate lifestyle activities in your life as well as regular cardiovascular exercise?

_____

_____

_____

Do you usually get a good night's sleep?

_____

_____

_____

How is your spiritual life? Do you have a regular practice? Do you
practice in a spiritual community?

_____

_____

_____

Your cave

Describe your home. How do you feel upon returning home—
calm? Restored? Grateful? Relaxed? Depressed? Overwhelmed? Do
you feel safe in your home? Can you be yourself?

_____

_____

_____

Your scent

What are the things that make you uniquely you? When someone
says, "She put her stamp on that," what are they seeing? When
someone says, "That's so *you*," what do they mean? If you left this
planet tomorrow, what would be missing? What would people
remember most about you?

_____

_____

_____

Your protection

Every animal has a way of defending itself against a threat. The
porcupine has its quills; the snake has its bite. When you need to
zing someone, how do you do it? Physically? (We hope not.) With
hurtful words? By retreating? Do you play opossum, pretending
you are dead? Or do you attack? Are you superior, condescending?

_____

_____

_____

At this point, we are not judging whether it's good or bad, positive or negative, just recognizing your natural tendencies. These protections may have developed for good reasons, but they may be based on old beliefs. We will examine these in subsequent chapters.

Your traps

Every animal has a weakness. The river trout is drawn to the fly, and so the fisherman can hook him. A hunter knows the shape of the deer's rib cage and the number of ribs. A hunter knows just where the heart is. What are your weaknesses? Another way of saying this is, "What are your buttons?" (If you don't know, ask your partner, family, or closest friends.) Awareness can help you stay intact when you perceive a threat—staying intact is a different animal from defending yourself.

_____

_____

_____

By stalking yourself, you lay the groundwork to take inventory of your mind. Once you cultivate this technique, you will become more aware of how your thoughts are creating the habitat of your spirit. You will ask: What am I thinking now? And then: Can I choose to think of something else?

Intuition in Massage

We all have an innate capacity for intuition. What Erica does when a client comes to her office may seem like magic, but the difference is that Erica has been cultivating her intuition about the body, mind, and spirit for many, many years. So she sees with a vision that surpasses that with which we operate in our daily lives.

You, too, come equipped with this knowledge, and the best way to unlock it is to begin to practice.

When the teacher is ready, the student appears.
—Buddhist saying

Collecting Intuitive Data

Erica is collecting data about a client long before the first phone call. Before she hears the voice on the phone, there has already been contact. What we mean by this is that somewhere in the collective unconscious, something has already been created that makes Erica and client connect. Erica has announced her receptivity; she is willing to be a healer to others who come seeking massage as a way to create body, mind, and spirit wholeness. The energy of that receptivity is out there, vibrating, seeking the new student.

Lest this sound just way too cosmic for you, let's look at it this way: Erica has an office. She has business cards. She has a sign on the street corner. She has clients who tell others about her technique, that it is unique, that an hour on her massage table is a quantum leap in consciousness. This is how the energy gets out there.

The second piece in bringing about a connection is the *intent* of the client. Someone who comes to Erica has already announced a desire for healing.

Touchstone: Sharing Energy

New Age massage recognizes that there is so much more to us than the skin, the muscles, the ligaments, the organs and bones that form our bodies. We are energy, and our energy fields extend beyond those bodies. In common parlance, this might be understood as "personal space," something that we develop a cultural understanding of as we are socialized. But of course, it is so much more than that.

In this exercise, sit across from your partner. Each of you holds up one hand as though hailing a taxi or giving a high five. Hold your hand about three inches from your partner's, so that you are palm to palm. What do you feel? Do you feel warmth? Do you feel a vibration?

Now hold up your other hand to your partner's. Did you feel the energy multiply?

Continue holding your hands up and together. Sit with the energy that is moving between you. Just feel it.

Often what people relate after trying this exercise is their awareness of the power of the intention to merge with another. This exercise is good practice in learning how to "hold someone," and by that we mean how to hold someone with honor and positive regard, with tenderness and awe in the magnificence of who they are. When we can *feel* that kind of energy in someone else, we no longer perceive that person as an outside force coming in. We can see that we are more alike than different. We can feel a bond. In that, there is great calmness.

If you like, take a few moments to make notes in your Empowerment Journal.

Beginning to know your body is beginning to know yourself. Our bodies provide us with many clues about what might be imbalanced. These indicators include sore muscles, muscle spasms, protective or fearful body language, facial expressions, voice inflections, and stillness versus nervous activity. These are all the first clues Erica uses when she begins to work with a client.

Pieces of the Puzzle

The next pieces of the intuition puzzle are in the voice and body language of the client. Then Erica does a mini-counseling session before the massage. With a highly tuned sense of intuition, Erica is picking up millions of bits of data.

On the phone, she notices if the client's voice is strained, rushed, calm, or shaky. She can hear the tears. She can hear the yearning for a calmer, saner life. She can sense the busy, frenetic schedule that creates the box someone may feel he is in. Body language provides more clues. Is the client holding her head up high or pulling inward? Is the client in a protective stance or an expansive, open stance?

When Erica asks a client how he has been feeling, if he says "nervous," for instance, she will ask where in his body he is feeling it. Our bodies are the seats of our emotions.

Catch and Release: An Emotional Check-In

It may seem easy to identify emotions, but truly it is quite difficult for many of us. Doing so requires us to open up. It requires us to drop out of the chatter of our thoughts and experience the feelings behind them. It requires us to take the risk that someone will say, "Don't feel that way."

A good practice is do an emotional check-in periodically throughout a day. You may opt to do this alone or with a partner. A good goal is to do this a few times in the morning, afternoon, and evening. Doing this will keep you mindful of your emotions. It will get you in practice for articulating them.

Ask yourself, "What am I feeling?" Start with these five words to describe your emotions: happy, sad, mad, fearful, ashamed.

You need do nothing. The rules are catch and release. You are neutral about your emotions. They are neither good nor bad. You just have them. Your goal is to get in the practice of noticing them.

Ray of Light: Deep Listening

One way Erica brings intuition to a massage is through deep listening. Recently, she met with a client we'll call Diana. After the pre-massage counseling, Diana requested an eye pillow or towel over her eyes. Erica remembered that Diana had mentioned several things had been coming up for her about her eyesight. Diana, about 40, was becoming far-sighted and had recently gotten no-line bifocals. She had mentioned a concern about macular degeneration (a disease of the eyes), though there was no history of it in her family. Diana also had mentioned she was operating at a high level of intellectual activity, and this was mentioned with both awe and concern. Diana was entering a new stage of life and had touched upon the many new ventures that were presenting themselves to her.

Erica honed in on Diana's need for creating a new vision for her life. This part of her body was being overtaxed, and she needed to balance it with groundedness. When Erica massaged Diana's ankles, she sensed an extraordinary sensitivity in that area—a neglected part of her body. Erica suggested Diana cultivate more movement, perhaps with dance. Diana mentioned an interest in ethnic dancing, such as Greek folk dances or Irish step dancing. In the same breath she mentioned though she had tried it recently, her feet were clumsy. "It's like my mind can't tell my feet what to do," she said. "I wanted to get to the point where my feet just knew." Erica noted she was right on track: It wasn't something her mind needed to tell her feet. She needed to tap into the energy in her feet, and let her feet learn the steps.

Touching the Calm Center

You, too, possess the intuition to pick up these cues. Have you ever told someone about a conversation you had with another person and found yourself saying, "I don't know, I just thought she seemed brusque." If quizzed further, you couldn't pinpoint it in something she said. But you knew on an intuitive level that you might have pushed a button with that person.

Intuition is that feeling of "I know, but I don't know *how* I know." That is the first step, but as you work with it and become clear in body, mind, and spirit, you will feel when the thought drops into your mind. With practice, you will know how you know. The more we listen to it, the more finely honed it can be.

Intuition can play a vital role in awakening your personal power, and it goes hand-in-hand with massage. Intuition is about knowing your body. It can be the first line of defense against stress. Stress management gurus teach us to identify three levels of stress:

1. **Mildly irritating.** This is the point at which you just take it in stride. It's not a roadblock, just a bump in the road.

2. **Bummer.** You recognize it as a bad event or a bad day. You may take time out to regroup but you don't make major changes.

3. **Screaming match.** It feels like life has tackled you, and the whole team is piling on. You finally hit critical mass. You hit the roof.

The first thing a stress management guru will tell you is that stress is a part of life. We don't make stress go away; we learn to manage it. A stress expert also will tell you that it's not what is happening to you but how you respond to external events that makes all the difference.

The role intuition plays in stress management is heightening your awareness of when you advance from one stage to another. An activated awareness of your thoughts can alert you to when you need to "snap out of it." As you develop your intuition, you'll listen to your body's signals. The more intuitive you become, the more quickly you'll be aware when you slip out of that state of centeredness.

By the same token, the more you cultivate that calm center within you, the more you will know what life is supposed to feel like. When you are experiencing stress in the same old way, in reactive mode, it will start to feel unnatural to you.

We are all equipped with this awareness. We are all equipped with that calm center within us that brings us the peace we desire.

Chapter 2

Acknowledge Your Divine Nature

It may seem in our time that healing is ubiquitous. You may meet people who swear by their massage therapist or their chiropractor. You may know people who use Chinese herbs or Bach's flower essences regularly, or maybe you know people who load up on echinacea, goldenseal, or grapefruit extract to fight off colds. Alternative medicine practices such as acupuncture are increasingly being embraced—and covered by insurance—in the realm of Western medicine. We use aromatherapy in our cars, and we use feng shui principles in arranging our homes. Healing-speak has seeped into the mainstream parlance in myriad ways. People—not just Californians—go around talking about "owning their stuff" and "being authentic." People don't just hang out anymore; they are "on a journey." Checking in with a friend, you might hear her refer to a confidence as "speaking my truth." If you click with someone, he might say, "That really resonated with me." If all this newfound gentleness and searching has you wondering what we are all trying to heal from, you are probably not the first.

We think it is this: *We are trying to heal from not knowing who we really are.*

Remember the movie *The Lion King?* Carolyn does. Vividly. She has four-year-old twins who can easily watch it three times in one week. In that movie, the lion Simba receives a message from his father from the Great Beyond, in which his father appears as a constellation in the night sky urging Simba to take his place as the rightful king. "Remember who you are," Mufasa says.

What we must remember is our Creator, our Source. What we must learn is our connection to it—and our part in it. This is the empowerment. New Age massage, combined with breath work, can open us to this experience of oneness. It can guide you in seeing your life from the viewpoint of the divine nature within you. Life, then, can take on a whole new meaning.

In this book, we recognize there are many paths. What you have come to believe about the One who created you as you are and what name you call Him/Her are *your* personal path. What we do want to guide you in is the many ways massage can lead you back to your Source, to see yourself outside the box of your daily life, to see your less-than-kind or imprisoning thoughts.

Just as there are many ways to experience the Divine, there are many ways to experience massage. Whether it's Native American hot-stone massage or Japanese-style Shiatsu massage, what is common to all traditions is a deep reverence for the body. New age massage is a blending of those traditions, and we see its emergence as a deep urge from humanity to experience greater ease with the truth of who we are.

What the traditions of different cultures bring to massage is that recognition of how connected our bodies are to nature, to each other and the Divine. That connection is honored as sacred.

When we seek out what is sacred, there is no other result but to heal.

The Many Paths to Healing

Why are there so many ways to heal? Why are there so many paths in? We think the answer is as simple as this: It's built into the design that we will find healing, that we will experience the magnificence of the divine nature within us. Being disconnected from it is very painful.

Traditions from India, China, Japan, Western Europe, Mexico, and the American Southwest are like different languages describing the way in to the temple of the sacredness of all life. Perhaps one will make sense for you at one time of your life; another will make sense for you at a different juncture of your life. Erica likens it to the tones of an Andes reed pipe. Each pipe is a different length. When sounded, each has a different tone. Each vibrates at a different level.

We think we are living in a special time, when we have access through the global village, through cyberspace, to explore the wisdom collected through the ages.

The traditions that we will explore in this book represent metaphors humanity has used to explain the way our bodies were created. All represent the different windows we have on seeing the world. Some cultures were the first to sense the chakras, areas of energy that reside along the spine and move through the top of the head, and that's what was recorded. The wisdom of chakra knowledge became incorporated into massage techniques that were handed down through time. Others, such as traditional Chinese medicine, were the first to sense the way the life force energy of ch'i flows through our bodies. Meridians are the way that energy is connected through our bodies.

You may already be aware that some techniques are common to different massage traditions. For instance, both Native American and Japanese massage have used hot stones for centuries. What we conclude from this is that in cultures where intuition is not blunted, it can seek out and attain the same place, even if those cultures are quite literally worlds— and ages—apart.

Empowerment Exercise: Glittering Sand

Begin by sitting comfortably on a pillow on the floor with your legs crossed. Hold your spine in a relaxed but straight position. Make sure you are not a ramrod. Straighten, then take a deep breath to settle in.

Breathe in and out through your mouth three times, exhaling as much as possible, so that you are empty of any old, stale breath.

Now shift your focus to your spine. With the next inhalation, see in your mind's eye a glittery thread of sand rising up the left side of your spine. As you exhale, see the glittery sand cascade down the right side of your spine. For eight minutes, maintain the rhythm of your breath, and focus on the glittering sand rising and falling. As other thoughts come, note them. Don't fight them or push them away; also don't keep them or dwell on them. Use the focus of the rising, glittering sand to bring you back.

Dwell now for two more minutes on that dazzling light inside you. Feel the sparkle move within you. Feel the warmth, feel the glow, as the sand massages you.

Now, with the next inhalation, see yourself in a desert. It is the end of the day, when the sun is its strongest, just about to set. The sand is glittering all around you. Keep breathing as you see yourself walking to the peak of a sand dune. Feel the glittering sand swirling around you. Feel the hot sun on your cheeks. As you scale the sand dune, feel the presence of others on the paths around you, ahead of you, behind you. Feel a prayerful benevolence envelop you. It is not just you. There are so many others on the glittering path.

> From the beginning of my life, I have been looking for your face. But today I have seen the charm, the beauty, the unfathomable grace of the face I was looking for. ... I am bewildered by the magnificence of your beauty and wish to see with a hundred eyes. My heart has burned with passion and has searched forever ... I am ashamed to call this love human and afraid of God to call it divine.
>
> —Rumi, thirteenth-century Persian poet and mystic

Ray of Light: Meeting the Divine

A client we'll call Stephanie came for a massage/breath session. She was feeling inundated by challenges: taking care of an aging mother, raising teenagers, keeping her marriage intact. She and her husband of 26 years were fighting constantly. But mostly she felt lost. Erica asked her, "What do you want for yourself?" Stephanie was unclear. The only thing she knew anymore was taking care of others. She had lost track of herself.

Preceding the first session, Stephanie and Erica did only a little sharing because Stephanie felt she was so close to a breakdown. Erica sensed that the time was now. The energy of Stephanie's divine nature was ready to move.

Erica led Stephanie in three breaths, then she began rocking Stephanie's body and touching different trigger points. Within 10 minutes Stephanie was experiencing waves of movement inside her body—intense sensations running up and down her body. Intense rage and sadness erupted through her body, released as tears, then pounding on the table. Then Stephanie laughed. She laughed and laughed and laughed with hearty belly laughs.

After about 40 minutes of breathing and releasing as Erica worked different parts of Stephanie's body, Stephanie spoke of the beautiful colors she was seeing and described an exquisite feeling infusing her body. It was deep joy. Then Stephanie said, "Oh my God, oh my God, oh my God!!"

After this, she settled, drifting into a state of peace and relaxation. Thereafter, Stephanie came for weekly sessions for three months. She kept coming until she felt complete.

The Web of Life

In *The Lion King*, Simba must go back to the prideland and face his past to take his place in the circle of life. He believes his father is dead, that he caused the death/separation and that he is cut off from the circle of life. But the Rafiki character (a baboon with medicine man wisdom) tells Simba he is mistaken, that his father is alive. "No," Simba says. "He died a long time ago." But Rafiki tells Simba his father is alive. He shows Simba his own reflection in a pool of water. "That's not my father," says a de-jected Simba. "It's just my reflection." No, says Rafiki, look closer. "Your father lives. Through you."

Wisdom, pain, courage, lack, grace, power, sadness, joy are passed down from grandmother to mother, from father to son, from Creator to Created. "We are all connected," Rafiki says. The message: To take our place in the circle of life, we must remember who we are. We must find our place.

In the song "Circle of Life" from *The Lion King*, the lyrics speak of the power of the circle of life to guide us toward taking our place on a path. The path before us unfurls into a circle, revealing how discovering our true purpose fits us into the bigger circle of life.

Central to Native American thought is that all life forms are connected. All living things—humans, animals, plants—are equal and are to be treated with equal reverence. Native American spirituality believes we are connected to our Creator through all life, and we maintain that connection through thankfulness. Gratitude, not petition or intercession, infuses Native American ceremonies. This sacredness will be our first stopping point as we explore the many traditions that influence the healing techniques of massage.

Touchstone: Mother Earth Shrine, the Sacredness of All

For just one day, as you go through your daily activities, collect 10 objects that remind you of the sacredness of all life. It may be most interesting to do this not on a weekend day, but an ordinary day when you are working, commuting, going to meetings—the whole swirl of life. This is when we are least likely to be mindful of the sacred, so this seems like the best place to begin to practice.

Be mindful throughout the day of the small joys of the natural world. Each time you notice, give thanks. Collect something that reminds you of that moment. It may be a dandelion, a maple leaf, a smooth stone, a sprig of rosemary, a ladybug, a tuft of rabbit fur left in the branches of a bush, a spider web. Throughout the day, keep the small objects in your pocket or on your desk. Touch them to remind yourself, to keep yourself mindful of the moment.

Map of the Heart

What you collect during your day of noticing the sacredness of life may be something you experience, but can't carry with you or put in a bottle. In that case, if the sky is a particularly inspiring shade of blue or a brooding shade of purple/slate, take the time to render that color in your Empowerment Journal. If you hear the coo of a dove, the purr of a cat, the rush of the wind through the trees, take a moment to record in your journal how that sound feels to you.

At the end of the day, you will assemble these items on your bureau or a small table in your home. This will be your shrine to the sacredness of all life. Remember to come back to it regularly. Take the time when you do to touch each item gently. Each time you find you need to reconnect to the sacredness of all life, assign yourself another day of collecting.

True Light

Once you can see the divine nature within you and be comfortable with that, you will experience a shift. Don't get us wrong, this is a tall order. It is much easier said than done. You may spend a lifetime trying to get it down, but it will be a wonderful journey.

It is so hard to see how we might possess within us the seed of the Divine, because most of the time, we feel so bounced around. Instead of experiencing our lives as we want them to be, we are just reacting to what's right in front of us. When we feel like we are controlled from outside, it can feel overwhelming to respond to a deeper, higher call. And when we get a glimpse of the Divine, we can only see that we are falling short.

After a while, we learn that all of the things that we seek for satisfaction don't work. Maybe first it was sex, drugs, and rock 'n' roll. Then it was herbs, chiropractors, and acupuncture. Those things work for a while, but then we are still reacting. It is when you get to the point that you know you don't want to go on this way that you can crack open the armor just a little bit to let some light in.

And once you do, you will see that what you were shutting out—the true light of the Divine in you—is not overwhelming. It is empowering. You begin to treat yourself with tenderness. As you let the light of the Divine take up more and more and more space within you, you begin to feel empowered.

> Our deepest fear is not that we are inadequate. Our deepest fear is that we are powerful beyond measure.
>
> —Marianne Williamson, spiritual leader and author, often attributed to Nelson Mandela, who used it in his 1994 inauguration speech

Empowerment Exercise: Honoring the Sacred

In Japanese Shiatsu massage, it is vital to first ground yourself. Many Shiatsu massage sessions take place on the floor. Being aware of gravity's effect on our physical bodies is the first step in opening oneself up to experience the sacred.

We will take a cue from Shiatsu and begin this exercise by bowing, a symbol of respect in Eastern cultures. You and your partner will kneel on the floor, using cushions if it makes you more comfortable. Bring your palms together at the chest level with your arms slightly extended. Relax and exhale. As you inhale, imagine the energy of the Divine flowing down through your hands. Exhale slowly and dip your head while opening your hands in a symbolic offering. Inhale and return to the starting position.

On your next exhalation, fold forward at the hips. Separate your hands, palms down, and place them on the floor. Let your forehead touch the ground. Keep breathing. Clear all thoughts.

After a few moments, inhale, returning to an upright position. Imagine energy from heaven breathing into you.

For the second part of the exercise, choose an object that holds sacred meaning for you. It could be a stone, a cross, a smudge stick, a golden leaf, a crystal. Share with your partner the significance of the object. Explain why it opens up your mind to the experience of the God of your understanding.

Together, take three deep breaths. Keep your eyes closed as you calm the mind and invite the breath of life within the safe place inside you. Hold it there as if it is a precious vase. Hold it in your mind's eye.

Extending your arm, hold the object out over the other's heart. As you do, say, "I now honor the sacred in you, as you were created." Now think of three things about your partner that you hold sacred. An example might be: "I now honor in you the sacredness of your smile, your laughter, and your joy, as you were created." Say it out loud. After you have said your three things, say, "I honor the Divine in you."

When you are done, switch roles.

We are, each of us, angels with only one wing; and we can only fly by embracing one another.
—Luciano De Crescenzo, Italian author and philosopher

Healing the Rift

If we can begin to see the sacredness in everything, we have taken the first step to take ourselves out of duality. There is no right or wrong, good or bad, light or dark, there is only oneness. In this place there is total acceptance. The more of this we can accept, the more of ourselves we can accept. The need to find some part of our selves right and other wrong diminishes. We move more into alignment with the truth of what we are. This would translate to fewer horrors and sorrows in the reality of our world. Heal the rift in our selves, and we heal the rift in the world.

Ray of Light: Darkness and Light

Diana, who we introduced in Chapter 1, came to Erica with the intent to heal some of her past relationships. She had struggled with the darkness in two men who had been in her life, and she was still hurting from the pain they had caused her.

Erica did some deep tissue work through Diana's neck and spine. Far into the session, with Diana doing some cleansing breath work, Erica cupped her hand over Diana's left eye. Diana related to Erica that she saw an egg held over her eye, split evenly in black and white. As Diana breathed through it, the white spread over the black, dissolving it. She reported that she saw in her mind's eye white particles falling from the "egg" to her sexual chakra (more about chakras in Chapter 4), then spiraling up in white cords back to her eye. The way Diana related this to Erica was, "I was saying to them, 'I can see your darkness. I can see your light. I can look at both sides of you, and not look away.'"

Diana's experience of being able to look unflinchingly at the darkness—and the light—in another is great progress. We fail to see our own divine nature because of the flaws we see within ourselves or others. Just the same, we can shrink from seeing the light within because its magnificence is just too scary.

What Lies Behind, What Lies Ahead

One of the earliest recorded mentions of massage is in Huang Ti Nei's "The Yellow Emperor's Classic of Internal Medicine," in third century B.C.E. China. We know that ancient Egyptians used massage because it is depicted in tomb paintings as far back as 3000 B.C.E. In ancient Persia, the physician Avicenna (980–1037 C.E.) wrote that massage relieved fatigued muscles. In India, massage has always played an important part in ayurvedic medicine, dating back more than 3,000 years. "Ayur-Veda," a sacred

Hindi book written about 1860 B.C.E., describes massage to reduce fatigue and promote well being.

Out of Chinese thought comes the philosophy of cultivating better physical, mental, and spiritual health by enhancing your life force energy—ch'i—and restoring balance. This philosophy permeates Taoism, Buddhism, and Confucianism. The concept of ch'i is central to acupuncture, feng shui, and yin/yang. It is vital to the discipline of movement—Tao Chi, qigong, and martial arts.

Traditional Chinese medicine focuses on correcting imbalances in the body, and so does ayurvedic medicine, which defines the body through types: *pitta* (Fire), *vata* (Air), and *kapha* (Water). Ayurveda believes that every human being is created from two energies. *Purusha* is pure consciousness, unexpressed and unknowable, the latent force of nature or choiceless passive awareness. It is parallel to the Chinese concept of yin. *Prakriti* is manifestation, creation, the principle of desire. *Prakriti* is choiceful active consciousness, and it is parallel to yang. Ayurvedic practitioners work with a system broken down into 10 pairs of opposites. These pairs are used in identifying tendencies and imbalances in diet, skin tone, emotional constitution, and activity. Examples of pairs might be: heavy/light; sharp/dull; hot/cold; mobile/static. Each ayurvedic client is profiled based on these pairs of opposites.

Eastern traditions, as well as Toltec traditions, operate on a higher awareness of energy fields that surround us, move through us, settle in us—whether it is ch'i in traditional Chinese medicine, chakras in Hindu thought, or awareness of auric fields in Toltec wisdom. Two massage techniques developed in Japan out of the Chinese concept of ch'i. Shiatsu, which quite literally means "finger pressure," was developed in twentieth-century Japan by Tamai Tempaku. Shiatsu's aim is to release trapped ch'i in the meridians through acupressure. Reiki is a practice that focuses on redirecting the energy fields in and around the body. In Japanese, the word means "universal life energy." A Reiki practitioner may lay her hands on the body or may hold her hands above the body, channeling healing energy into the body. Touch is held for a long time, usually three to five minutes.

Each school of thought represents different views of the Divine, of our bodies, minds, and spirits, but they hold many common beliefs. There are many parallels between the five Chinese elements and the five Native

American elements. In traditional Chinese medicine, the five elements are Fire, Wood, Metal, Air, and Water. In Native American thought, though elements and beliefs vary from tribe to tribe, primary elements are Earth, Wind, Fire, Air, and Great Spirit.

Distill these traditions, and you arrive at one core truth: *Touch heals.* A 1992 study conducted by the Touch Research Institute out of the University of Miami School of Medicine documented positive benefits of massage. According to the study, massage plays a strong role in relieving a list of afflictions from HIV, premature birth, emotional abuse, depression, eating disorders, drug addiction, cancer, asthma, diabetes, and on and on.

Another core truth is that relaxation triggers movement of energy through the channels within the body, which creates expansion—that is, the openness that allows for us to change and to heal. That expansion is an ever-increasing spiral, lifting us upward.

Ghost in the Machine

But this is what we are up against. Western thought conceptualizes each individual as a "ghost in the machine," a rational or Divine mind imprisoned in plodding, carnal flesh. In Western thought, we're really great, but the flesh is holding us back, and it is to be warred against. And war against it we do. In the name of attaining the American cultural ideal of beauty, too many of us starve, drug, or torture our bodies. Even those of us who have a more balanced view—who know better—are often very critical of our bodies, without realizing how cruel this can be to ourselves.

This, we believe, is the reason that much of the new thought has turned to Eastern philosophies for different ways of perceiving the body, one that is connected to the mind and spirit, one that holds more reverence for the package we come in.

Touchstone: Try a Little Tenderness

Do this exercise with your partner. He (or she) can lie on the floor, a sofa, bed, or massage table. Take in three cleansing breaths together. You are creating a space of wholeness. Within that you are creating tenderness. As you cup your hands over your partner's ears, breathe in gentleness and tenderness. As the two of you continue to breathe, each of you follows this visualization. Let the image of your bodies fall away in your mind. See your skin diffusing into the energy around you. See your muscles and tissues dissolve. See the bones soften. Hold it there, feeling only the energy of your essence and your partner's essence. As you hold your partner in tenderness, feel his innocence. Feel the gentleness increase in you as you feel his innocence expand.

When you switch places, and you are lying with your partner's hands cupped over your ears, notice how safe you feel.

Afterward, compare your experiences. Take a few moments to note them in your Empowerment Journal.

> And God created man in His own image, in the image of God, He created him; male and female, He created them.
> —Genesis 1:27

Remapping

Erica cannot count how many clients have commented to her over the years that massage has awakened a voice of a less-than-kind message once received. The touch and pressure of massage in certain areas of the body will spark a voice for a client. She will say, "Wow, that's my mother's voice," or he will say, "My grandfather always said that." This awakening is the first step to recognizing beliefs we may have but aren't conscious that we have. Clients will say, "I didn't know I always believed that. I've been fighting that all my life, and now I see where it comes from."

Facing the Past

In *The Lion King*, Simba hesitates to return to the prideland because he will have to face his past. Rafiki bonks him on the head. When Simba asks, "What did you do that for?" Rafiki replies, "What does it matter? It's in the past." Simba says, "Yeah, but it still hurts." When Rafiki moves to swing at him again, Simba blocks him. "The way I see it," says Rafiki, "you can either run from it or learn from it."

As you receive a massage, you may also awaken voices from your past. Where did the message that your nose was big or your chin too pointy come from? Where did you hear that you were not supposed to talk in a loud voice because it was unfeminine? Where did you hear that you were not a manly man? Once you discover where you first touched that thought and imprinted it on your body, mind, and spirit, it will no longer have power over you.

Empowerment Exercise: The Violet Flame

In this exercise with your partner, sit cross-legged on cushions on the floor, across from one another. Close your eyes and take three deep breaths. As you settle into your body, feel yourself grounded on the floor. You are being supported by Mother Earth, resting gently.

Now imagine within you, at your center, a violet flame. As you continue to breathe gently, breathe in through your nose and out through your mouth. Allow the violet flame to expand. With each breath, let the flame grow. Let it fill you. When you feel yourself filled with the flame, you will likely feel yourself enlivened and awakened throughout your body. Extend your hands and touch your partner's hands. Do not worry if you are the first to fill up with the violet flame. Extend your hands and wait, continuing to let the flame glow within and without.

When you have both touched this place, open your eyes. Your partner will extend her hands, palm up. Continuing breathing, reach out and gently trace your fingers over your partner's face. Move down the shoulders, tracing your hand down your partner's arms until your palms gently meld into your partner's.

Say, "When I see the Divine in you, I see the Divine in me. Thank you."

Now hold out your palms. Let your partner place his fingertips on your forehead, your cheeks, your chin, tracing them down your face. Let him touch your neck, your collarbone, your shoulders. Each touch should be with reverence. Breathe in your partner's reverence for you. If voices come in, note them, but don't dwell on them. Bring your focus back to your partner's fingertips. Bring your focus to your breathing and the space between your partner's fingertips and your skin. Let him trace his fingers down the length of your arms. Let him gently meld his palms into yours. Listen to him say, "When I see the Divine in you, I see the Divine in me. Thank you."

Your Higher Self

In a previous Ray of Light, Stephanie allowed herself to completely open to the feelings that her divine nature or higher self were bringing to her. She was allowing herself to be led. When this happens, it means we are asking for information from our higher self.

This just takes practice! The more you do it, the more natural it feels to constantly check in with what you are feeling in the moment. The more this infusion of divine nature and "human self" occurs, the less we are led around by our fear-based or imprisoning thoughts.

Divinity and Humanity

We are reminded of the poignant Easter homily delivered by the young priest in the movie *Chocolat*. The movie depicted a beautiful young woman, played by Juliette Binoche, who opened a confectionery of exquisite chocolates across the square from a Catholic church, just at the onset of Lent. The mayor of the French village strictly polices the villagers in resisting temptations during Lent, but ... well, you can guess what happens. The chocolates are too much to resist, even, eventually, for the mayor. On Easter Sunday, the priest (whose confessed weakness is American rock 'n' roll, as in Elvis Presley) stumbles through his homily, straying from his script. Instead, he announces that he prefers not to speak of the divinity of Christ, but rather His humanity, the way he lived on Earth. This is what fascinates him, what he implores the parishioners to embrace. The priest urges them to measure their goodness not by what they deny themselves and whom they exclude, but rather to measure their goodness by what they embrace, what they create, and who they include.

The purpose of using massage in healing is to create the space for goodness and wholeness. In creating oneness within—by what you embrace, by what you create, by what you include, by what you know is the truth about yourself—you create the space for all to be one: unity. As we begin to find unity within, we create a greater integrity of self. If we each do that, we have no more victims, no more perpetrators, no more evil, no more good. No more rampant greed, no more rampant rage. Instead: rampant joy.

Chapter 3

Mind, Body, and Spirit Meld

The unity of mind, body, and spirit is at the core of many of the traditions that influence new age massage. Wholeness is the starting point, as much as it is the goal. We believe the surge of interest in traditional Chinese medicine, ayurvedic medicine, and native spirituality stem from that deep desire to connect the mind and the spirit to what is happening in the body. As a people, we have felt it "in our bones," so to speak, for centuries. As a culture, we are just now coming to acknowledge it. In practicing it, we find it works. If it feels like it works, it does. We just have to trust in the process.

You are your own best healer. You possess inside you the best knowledge about your body and its well-being. Your instincts are your biggest asset.

In this chapter, we will draw upon the traditions of Chinese medicine, ayurveda, and other schools of thought about the mind, body, and spirit to teach you massage techniques that will activate your intuition.

The Origin of Pain

In Eastern philosophy, a headache is not just a pain in the head. It's not just something to be treated with an analgesic. Sure, after taking acetaminophen we feel better. The throbbing stops. But what caused the headache? What is its origin? In this way, new age massage poses the same questions. The aim is to get to the source of the pain.

Traditional Chinese medicine views pain as an obstruction of ch'i, the life force energy of the universe. Your body is an ever-shifting mosaic of energy fields, shifting in and out of balance. You are affected by your energy and also the energy around you, because we are all connected.

Ch'i is believed to arise from the interaction of the forces of yin and yang. Yin and yang are complementary yet interdependent opposites, like night and day. One flows into the other, becoming the other. They both create and influence each other. Within one is the seed of the other.

Yin is often thought of as feminine energy, while yang is masculine. Yin energy is receptive, while yang is direct action. Different organs of the body are ruled by yin energy or yang energy, and yin/yang energy flows through the body in channels called meridians. In Chinese medicine, the organs are connected in a sequence, so often if one organ is deficient, the practitioner treats the situation by strengthening the next organ in the sequence.

Why Yin When You Can Yang? Or Vice Versa ...

As complementary and interdependent energies, yin and yang both create and control each other. When yin declines, yang expands, and vice versa.

There are five key concepts of yin and yang, as explained in the following table.

Concept	Example
Opposition: Two forces are in a constant struggle with one another.	Acting/waiting
Mutual dependence: One cannot exist without the other.	Cloud/rain
Mutual consumption and support: Each gives of itself to support the other.	Cow/pasture
Inter-transformation: One becomes the other.	Night/day
Infinite subdivisibility: Each contains the seed of the other.	Joy/sadness

Take a few moments now to think of some yin/yang energy pairs and note them in your Empowerment Journal.

Tools in the Toolbox

If someone came to Erica complaining of chronic headaches, she might draw upon yin/yang energy in the way she treats him. She would know that the head is considered yang, while the feet are considered yin. She might then guide the client in visualizing the receptivity of yin as the client breathes through the massage session. She might spend more time massaging the client's feet, which are yin, to activate yin energy within the body. She might focus more on relaxation, because too much yang energy means the circuits of the body are strained. There is too much going out, not enough coming in to sustain and nourish.

Yin	Yang
Lungs	Large intestine
Spleen	Stomach
Heart	Small intestine
Kidneys	Urinary tract, bladder
Pericardium (sac surrounding the heart)	Triple burner (an organ function)
Liver	Gallbladder

Then again, Erica may turn to the concept of chakras that are derived from the Hindu tradition that gives us yoga and ayurvedic medicine. The seven primary chakra energy centers are each said to vibrate with a color, with energy rising up through a channel in the center of the spine and out through the head. Kundalini is the life force energy that rises through the spine. It is the attainment that comes when energy from the chakras is harmonized. Someone with a headache would have an imbalance more than likely in the sixth (thinking) chakra, located just above the eyebrows, centered between the eyes and about an inch deeper than the skin. This is sometimes called the third eye, and its color is indigo. Or someone with a headache that is centered on the crown might have an imbalance in the seventh chakra, or spiritual chakra, which is purple. When Erica uses the chakras to guide her in massage techniques, she works on the principle that chakras work conjointly. For instance, the sixth chakra (thinking) works in concert with the second chakra, which is the sexual chakra. She might massage the client's feet, which would allow the client to open to the slower rhythms of the body.

Another place Erica might turn to inform her techniques for a session is ayurveda. In ayurveda, energies are broken down into types:

- A *pitta* type is fiery, sometimes confrontational, always direct. A pitta has a lot of drive.
- A *vata* type is airy, light, vast, capacious, enlivened. A vata is a thinker.
- A *kapha* type is heavy, slow and sweet, more emotional. A kapha tends to process emotions slowly and tends to take on other's emotions. These people are often sedentary.

While ayurvedic types describe certain body types and certain personalities, the types can also apply to modalities of massage. For instance, the client with the headache may be a pitta type whose confrontational style and hard-driving approach have created an imbalance. Erica might use a lot of kapha techniques for that person. Think of kapha energy as thick molasses. Kapha strokes would be long, slow strokes, something that might be similar to what we know as Swedish massage.

On the other hand, if a kapha type came to Erica with lower back pain and chronic depression, and Erica knew the client had a sedentary lifestyle, Erica might apply vata techniques to open her mind and lift her spirit. The touch might emphasize sensation rather than depth. Erica might use Reiki techniques or apply polarities, the rebalancing of positive and negative energies. She might emphasize more breathwork.

Another vata technique draws upon the Native American massage technique of dry brushing. This technique, used by the Cherokee Indians, uses a dry brush over the body. While it exfoliates the skin, it stimulates circulation of the blood and lymphatic fluids, increasing vitality and enhancing the beauty of the skin. A pitta technique might be fast, deep pressure, or pressure that is quickly and firmly applied. Erica will use her thumbs or perhaps an elbow as she holds a point.

For very old, deep pain, Erica will employ kapha techniques. As she puts full weight, boring down into a muscle, she would move up very slowly to release the old pain. Or in the case of someone grappling with chronic depression and perhaps overweight due to a sedentary lifestyle, Erica may turn to a pitta technique, to activate the circuits so that more is going out and less energy is stored up. The client may be holding on, receiving too much, may feel too responsible for others. So Erica would try to use pitta techniques to release some yang energy in the body to balance the yin.

Touchstone: The Dance of Yin and Yang

Every massage is a dance of yang and yin, of stimulating techniques and calming techniques. Erica notes if the client is agitated or barely present, not in his body. If the person is agitated, she starts with calming techniques. If the person is too passive, she starts with stimulation.

The stimulating techniques flow into the calming techniques, in the same way the principle of mutual consumption works in yin/yang: Stimulation gives way to calmness. As Erica gives a massage, she is tuned in to the rise and fall of these energies, letting them decline and expand.

Put on some music that moves in this way, rising and falling. With your partner, practice some of the techniques described earlier.

The Greatest Tool: Your Intuition

All of these are just some of the tools in the toolbox of the massage therapist, but the greatest tool of all is your intuition about your body.

Getting to the point where you can hear what your body is telling you is a vital first step to healing. How can you train yourself to notice what you're feeling?

Ray of Light: Hearing Your Voice

Abby is an older woman who has been dealing with panic attacks and depression. She came to see Erica for 3 sessions in a 10-day period. Abby felt incredible pain during the first session, but it was good pain in that it served to move her forward. She was breathing through it and felt relief. She cried during the sessions, experiencing a lot of physical and emotional release.

The second time she came in, Abby had the sense during the session that she was giving birth. She said the pain felt like an entity in her body, moving through her.

On the third visit, Abby recalled a psychic told her once she "came from the star." She had never understood that. But by the third session, she had gone so deeply into her body and her intuition that she remembered as a child receiving visits from angels. She reported to Erica that she felt that same angelic presence in the room during the massage. The image in her mind was that she, Abby, was amid the stars. Erica directed her to breathe that into her body, anchoring it there. Abby experienced a shaking, tremulous release. Through the presence of the angel, she felt a long lineage of guidance and support from important men in her life who had passed on to the other side. In that session, Abby reclaimed her innate understanding of her way. She reclaimed it and felt incredibly empowered.

After the three-session sequence ended, Abby checked in with Erica by phone. Her voice sounded different, energized. Abby had very little pain. Even by her third session, she had been moving more freely and confidently. She had a bounce to her step.

Your sacred space is where you can find yourself again and again.
—Joseph Campbell, American author on mythology and comparative religion

Deeper into the Forest: An Intuitive Body Scan

This exercise picks up where the Stalking Yourself exercise in Chapter 1 left off. If you'll remember, in that exercise, we were hunters recording data about the prey, noting its habitat and scent—only *we* were the prey. Now we will learn more about this creature's habits of thought, the way those thoughts are stored in the body, and the way they can be released or restored through massage. You can do this exercise with a partner or alone.

You may want to put on some soothing, spiritual music as you do this exercise.

Lie down where you can be comfortable. Take in several relaxing breaths.

Bring your focus inside, just below your heart, to your center. As you work through this, keep breathing consciously.

We are going to take inventory, scanning the body for imbalances and blockages, places with trapped energy and pain. As you inhale, lift your focus to your forehead. Now imagine with each breath the muscles in your forehead relaxing, the tightness dissolving. Think of the many ways your forehead works for you. It is the thinking center, but it is also the indicator of your emotions. It shows your frowning, your scowling, your surprise, your listening and receptivity to new ideas, your happiness. Have you ever heard the phrase, "It was written all over her face?" Sometimes it *is* written right there. As you breathe, you are letting go, breath by breath, of everything that has ever been written.

As you move methodically down through the body, and as you leave one area behind, bless it. Thank that area for all that it does for you.

Continuing to breathe, move to the cheekbones, then the jaw. You'll move to the neck and shoulders, down the upper arms to the forearms, then the hands, relaxing each finger one by one. You may find that some parts are tighter than others, and you may need to linger there and breathe through them. You may want to say these out loud to your partner so he or she can make some notes in your Empowerment Journal.

Now move down through the torso, relaxing the abdomen, the pelvis. What do you notice next? A hollow sensation in the abdomen? Pressure in your intestines? Breathe through that area. Take a moment to see if you can tell what thought or emotion is sitting there. You may recall a scene, a conversation, a place. Wait, breathe and some clue will present itself. If it helps, say aloud, "I allow myself to know. I am not judging." You are not evaluating.

Now move on down the body, releasing the muscles in your thighs, your calves and finally your feet.

If sad thoughts or disturbing feelings arise as you do this, use your breath to push them out of you. Notice which organ or area of your body evoked the feeling. Blow the feeling up and away from you. See light coming into yourself and filling up the space left behind by the painful feeling.

When you are done, tell your body out loud, "Thank you."

If you have done this with a partner, switch roles.

Emotional Check-In

Were you surprised at the emotions, thoughts, and memories that came up during this exercise? Were you surprised at how they were connected to certain organs? Of course, some of the connections are more obvious, such as the heart and emotions.

In traditional Chinese medicine, it is believed that all organs are ruled by an emotion. For instance, it is believed that the kidney is where fear is stored, while anger is stored in the liver and worry in the spleen. Quite naturally, the heart is the center of joy. The lungs are ruled by sadness. The heart and lungs work together, just as joy and sadness have their own dynamic, one flowing into the other. The heart needs the lungs to renourish the oxygen in the blood and release the carbon dioxide that no longer nourishes the body. The lungs need the heart to infuse us with new energy to progress to the next level of joy.

In this instance, the yin and yang workings of the heart and lungs serve as a metaphor for releasing and letting go of old hurts and fears. We must release the carbon dioxide from our lungs—the sadness, the hurtful thoughts that no longer serve—to nourish the plants. The plants in turn nourish us, taking in the carbon dioxide and producing oxygen that nourishes us. So we *must* release.

Take a few moments to breathe in and out deeply and fully as you meditate upon the rising and falling of energy in your heart and lungs. Feel the breath massage you from within upon each inhalation and exhalation. Center until you feel the massaging rhythm of blood coursing through your body become gentle and grounded, flowing as a river through your tissue and muscles.

Don't Take the Poison

As you practice getting in tune with your body, you will learn to ask yourself throughout the day, "What seems out of balance? What do I need right now?" For too long, too many of us have not been letting our bodies speak the truth. We get that tight knot in the stomach, the tightness around the shoulders. We don't even realize it when it takes hold. We get so good at not noticing that it didn't feel right when a co-worker or family member said something mean, or that we thought something mean toward ourselves.

Speaking from the Toltec tradition, don Miguel Ruiz, author of *The Four Agreements*, calls this "taking the poison." When we are the recipients of cruel, insensitive, or misguided comments, we don't have to take it in and make it our story. One of the Four Agreements is "Don't take it personally." Other people who are out of alignment, who are not whole, are desperately trying to get us to take their poison. *What I have inside me is just too painful,* they think, *but if I can just get this away from me, I'll be okay.* If you take it in, you are taking in their self-hatred and their deep dis-ease with themselves.

This can happen without our ever realizing it. We have taken the poison when we let others' judgments or perceived judgments become our story about who we are. "I really should have a husband by now. After all, I'm 35," is an example—a message we might have gotten from a mother eager for grandchildren, a married friend living in suburban stay-at-home bliss, or the media, which tells us we should not be alone. "I really need to lose weight" is another. Or: "My wife is right. I am too passive."

Sometimes the feedback is useful. Maybe it's "I need to hold back my sharp tongue sometimes" or "I need to be a better listener." In cases like these, we may be shutting the message out for fear of having to see a flaw we need to correct to improve a relationship. Perhaps we fear being vulnerable or we fear changing.

Personal coach and author Martha Beck has an exercise she does with her clients. She sometimes makes her clients do pushups while reciting some of the "stories" they have been given about themselves. If the statement is false, the strength drains from their bodies. If it is true, they get fired up and start cranking out pushups. This is an excellent way of setting up an internal detector to evaluate feedback, welcome or otherwise, you have received about yourself. Shed yourself of the stories you no longer need. Take what you need and leave the rest.

Empowerment Exercise: Poison Purge

Together with a partner who knows you well, draw up a list of some of the negative things you believe about yourself. These may be based on feedback you have received whether you solicited it or not.

Here are some examples:

- I am a deficient spouse.
- I need to lose weight.
- I usually run late.
- I am an inadequate parent.
- I need to find a mate.
- I need to be a better listener.
- No one understands me.
- I should really just be bold sometimes. I am too passive.
- I have a few quirks.
- I am messy.
- I am not that good at setting boundaries.
- I am inconsiderate.
- I am loud.
- I am distant.
- I am not that disciplined about my work.
- I am not a sensual person.
- My needs don't matter.
- I am not that good at speaking my needs.
- I can't say no.
- I don't know anything about computers.
- I should really just let go sometimes. I am too intense.

Pick three or four that evoke the strongest reaction for you. How do you know? These are the three or four you would spend the most time talking about with another friend over coffee, as in, "and then—you won't believe this—he said I was messy. Messy? Can you believe that?"

Now you are going to do pushups as you say each aloud. If you are not strong enough to do full pushups, you can do them on your knees. If that also proves difficult, put your palms at shoulder width against a wall and do pushups against the wall from a standing position (or you can do this seated in a chair, if you need to). Have your partner observe you. Are you getting stronger? Are you getting weaker? How is the massaging movement of exercise energy depleting or enriching?

Take some time to make some notes in your Empowerment Journal.

There's Magic Ahead

To know your body intuitively, you must take the step of allowing your body to open and empty. That is why Erica begins a massage session with three deep breaths that empty out the old stale air and bring in new. She tells clients to think of creating an open space in their abdomens and fill it up with new.

Breath and massage have a purifying effect. It's your perception that it's poison, but in fact, it's a transmutation. We don't so much purge the poison as much as we change it. The first step is becoming mindful of it. Don't deny that another person's judgments of you are painful; allow yourself to be in it, to see what it has to say. Sometimes the poison gets our attention so we can change it to an expansion instead of a contraction.

In Buddhism, this practice is *tonglen,* the art of transforming impurities. We breathe in the negative energy, and the body purifies it. We breathe out love. In this view, not only does the negativity inform, if we are mindful, but the body and breath itself transform the energy.

When we talk about stalking yourself or finding the stillness within, no matter the culture, no matter the tradition, the direction is the same: inward. The key is to know yourself, because the information you have inside is vital to transformation and purification. At some point, a client will say to Erica, "It's time to go inside." This comes after the statement of intent, "I want to feel alive. I want to feel peace." Once you stake out the inner territory, the space opens up for a synchronistic energy to work in an assertive way to bring events, people, and experiences designed to move you ahead. The magic begins to happen.

Map of the Heart

In your Empowerment Journal, write a stream of consciousness about what is limiting you. What are the barriers to your dreams? What is stopping you from feeling good? What, if only it could happen for you, would change it all? Just write for 10 minutes without stopping. Don't stop. Keep the pen moving. Don't evaluate what you are writing. It's not stupid. No one will see it.

It's like a garden hose clogged with muck. To clean out the muck, we will run water through it. At first, all that comes out is sludge, then clogs of dirt. Then it's muddy water, and then it runs clear.

Do this 10 minutes each day for a week. Notice how the water runs clear after a while.

Aligning with Discernment

In the Toltec tradition, as a person stalks self-knowledge, the next step is discernment. Discernment is the beginning of sifting out the old knowledge that doesn't serve you well from the new knowledge that can power you forward. People ask Erica, "How can I know which voice to trust?"

It's easy to see why we aren't immediately sure. After all, we have plenty of experiences to look back on with 20/20 hindsight where we can see that heeding our thoughts and acting on what seemed like a gut feeling at the time wasn't such a good idea after all. Ask any divorced person whether he or she would agree "love is blind," and you know what we mean.

It is true that it's hard to know which voice to trust. In the preceding exercises, we have worked to clarify your inner voice so you can clean out the gunk. Honing your intuition means distilling your inner voice down to its very truest essence.

We have talked about the "poison" of other people's gunky thoughts and the energy that can get stored inside our bodies as a result. You may wonder if it's such a good idea to tap into the collective unconscious, as described by psychologist Carl Jung. Maybe, you wonder, it's polluted.

The first step toward discernment is taking responsibility for our thoughts. When Erica works with a client over time, she works with that person through a massage session to collect and discern his thoughts as they come up. The first question she trains the client to ask is, "Where does this thought come from?" Does it come from the gunk? Or does it come from a higher place? What pattern does it show you about yourself? What belief do you realize you are holding in your subconscious?

Over time, a client who has been through many massage therapy sessions with Erica will have stored in his or her body the knowledge of the higher level of thought. During a massage, as old stuff is released, new breath and new life energy are stored in the body. So the body starts to know, too, what is coming from the higher level of thought, free of the reactivity of the past.

The Hunting Ground: Stalking Discernment

Just as the hunter would discern whether the hunted was a one kind of deer or another, we want to know the kind of animal we are dealing with. Know that there are two types of thoughts—those that come from outside you that you may have taken in without weighing their merits, and those that come from the Origin or Source, the Divine, or God of your understanding. So ask yourself, is this a thought that comes from the mass of humankind, as in one of the most prevalent thoughts of the culture? Or does it come to me as an original thought?

When we begin to take responsibility for our thoughts, we start tracking their origins. We can start being aware of our unconscious reactions. Once we empower ourselves to observe the thought and the reaction to the thought, we have the power to determine if this is what we really want. Is this really working for me?

Now you can claim the responsibility for your actions.

Through massage, done in conjunction with breath, we lay the hunting ground to allow all of this information and new understanding to reveal itself. Think of the hunter waiting in a blind for the deer to emerge in the clearing in the forest.

Within my body are all the sacred places of the world, and the most profound pilgrimage I can ever make is within my own body.
—Saraha, Buddhist master

Empowerment Exercise: Emulating the Rabbit, Sasangasana

In yoga, the practitioner moves into poses that emulate the spirit she is beckoning in. The movements are designed to put the practitioner in the frame of mind to draw into herself the essence of that energy: the Child pose, the mountain, the lightning bolt. In this respect, yoga can be thought of as internal massage. Asanas, or postures, are thought of as opening energy centers and chakras in the body.

In this asana, you are assuming the form of the rabbit, the hunted. Begin in Child's pose: Kneel with your forehead touching the floor and your arms at your sides, reaching toward your feet. Now, holding on to your heels, move your forehead to your knees and the crown of your head to the floor. Continuing to hold tightly to your heels, inhale and move your hips up to the ceiling. Breathe. Hold the pose for four to eight breaths. Notice how the breath massages and relaxes your body. Notice as well areas of tension in this pose and breathe into them as you assume the shape and form of the rabbit. Now relax into Child's pose.

Yoga's Rabbit pose moves you into a space of innocence and vulnerability, but also evokes the rabbit's agility.

Empowerment Exercise: Vision Quest

In Native American spirituality, the vision quest is used as a practice for releasing the old and embracing a new level of consciousness. In it, the practitioner must quite literally lose herself to find herself. All of the old thought forms must be left behind. The approach is to purge them out of the body. This may be done by fasting. Or it is sometimes done with days of group chanting or drumming. These serve to put you in a meditative state in the moment. The simple, repetitive rhythm shuts out all old thoughts, creating a space for the new, anchoring you in the moment. The power of community is vital, too; it is the collective force of all the chanters and drums that can move this bad energy out of you. Sometimes, it is done in a sweat lodge, to sweat out all the toxins from the body. Sometimes, it is done by walking on fire. Through all of these methods, the aim is to purge and purify. The old self dies. A new being emerges.

After completing a vision quest, the person participates in a ceremony to learn and receive his sacred name. The name is a symbol of your true power self, a self that is divinely inspired, without the limiting fear thoughts that continue to hold you in your small self.

Purification can come in small steps. It is vital that as you take these steps toward purification, you call in the protection of the Divine. As you move into releasing impurities, fear comes up in the body. It may be fear of the unknown, fear of not doing it right, fear of releasing something out of your control, fear of darkness. Do not allow yourself to stay with the fear, because you will continue to attract these things.

With a partner, sit together with a metal bowl between you. Each of you has paper and pencil. Take a few minutes to thank Love or Holy Spirit or the Divine for being with you and guiding your release this evening. Know that you are protected and inspired by this Divinity. Say together, "We are safe." Both of you will write down on the pieces of paper any and all fears that you have about a certain subject or issue that is up for you. Keep going until you run out of fears. Take turns reading a fear out loud and burn the paper in the metal bowl. When each person completes the stack of fears, say, "Thank you. We are released, we are cleansed, we are healed. And so it is."

I have come all this way for you without shoes or shawl.
—Rumi, thirteenth-century Persian poet and mystic

Elemental Healing: Purification

For deep, lasting healing to take place, you must get to the essence. You must strip to the core: purify, purify. Heat is powerful. It can dislodge old negative beliefs. It can purify. There is creative deconstruction in the power of fire. Fire blazes upward. It becomes something else—ash and air.

The role of heat in massage is primarily to soften and open the soft tissue, but it also opens the organs—liver, kidneys, spleen, stomach, diaphragm. When the soft tissue of the body is open and warm, the toxins can rise in the tissue and loosen. Then by stimulating circulation, the toxins or trauma can be removed from the tissue. The tissue can then heal or mend itself by cells reproducing themselves in the proper way.

Touchstone: Friction

A great way to create heat in the body is to create friction. Hold your partner's foot in your hand by holding your hand over the top of her foot and keeping all the toes steady with your hand. Then with your other hand, rub vigorously up and down on the sole of her foot. Do it until her foot becomes hot. Repeat with the other foot. Then trade places. This should feel very comforting.

Chinese Elemental Healing

The elements of life are the building blocks for healing. In traditional Chinese medicine, the five elements are sometimes called the five transformations or five phases, signifying the journey toward healing. The five Chinese elements mirror those of the Native American elements and those of common parlance: Earth, Water, Fire, and Air. But let's take a closer look at what these traditions believe about the elements.

The five Chinese elements are Water, Fire, Wood, Metal, and Earth. Each element is connected with a yin organ and a yang organ, an emotion, a season, and a color. Each rules certain body tissues and fluids. For instance, Fire rules the blood vessels and sweat. Its yin organ is the heart, while its yang organ is the small intestine. Fire rules the sense of taste; its sound is laughter, and its emotion is joy.

Element	Wood	Fire	Earth	Metal	Water
Color	Blue/green	Red	Yellow	White	Black
Symbol	Dragon	Phoenix	Caldron	Tiger	Tortoise
Season	Spring	Summer	Transition (Vernal and autumnal equinox; winter and summer solstice)	Autumn	Winter
Months	December	April, May	March, June, September, December	July, August	October, November
Weather	Rain	Heat	Wind	Clear	Cold
Direction	East	South	Center	West	North
Planet	Jupiter	Mars	Saturn	Venus	Mercury
Day	Thursday	Tuesday	Saturday	Friday	Wednesday
Sense	Sight	Taste or speech	Touch	Smell	Hearing
Yin organ	Liver	Heart	Spleen	Lungs	Kidneys
Yang organ	Gallbladder	Small intestine	Stomach	Large intestine	Bladder
System	Nervous	Circulatory	Digestive	Respiratory	Excretory
Emotion	Anger	Joy	Worry	Sadness	Fear
Body	Nerves	Blood	Muscles	Skin	Bone

You can see the intuitive connections. The heart is the receptacle for joy. Its expression is laughter. In some texts, Fire rules not taste but speech. Speech is the way we connect through the heart, but it is also the way we can flame others, hurting them with our words. That Fire rules the blood vessels and sweat makes sense, because those represent the life force surging through us constantly. It also makes sense that Fire is the force that purges blood and sweat from our bodies when we are put to the test.

How could that translate to massage? If Erica knows that a client needs to evoke more laughter in her life, she may tap into connectivity of the Fire element, knowing that stimulation to the circulatory system, the heart and the small intestine are key to opening up blockages to joy. As she considers which pressure points to use, she may chose ones that open up those meridians. This worked, for instance, in the Ray of Light with Stephanie in Chapter 2, when Stephanie's pain erupted into hearty belly laughs.

By contrast, the elements of the ancient Anasazi culture in the Native American Southwest are Earth, Water, Air, Fire, and Great Spirit. Earth, Water, Air, and Fire form a great circle, in which Great Spirit is the center. It is believed Anasazi chose the locations of their sacred spots based on these elements, with Great Spirit at the center. In the city of Albuquerque, the Petroglyph National Monument runs along the western rim of the city, where there are five dormant volcanoes. Amid the black lava rocks there are many sacred petroglyphs that indicate this may have been the center of the Great Spirit. The sites of other petroglyphs north, south, east, and west around New Mexico, and their distance from this site point to this as the center. The Anasazi never would have lived at a sacred site, and there is no evidence of any permanent settlement in this area, as there are in others.

Different tribes, from Navajo to Hopi to Pueblo to plains Indians, hold different beliefs about the elements, directions, and their meanings. Many of the ceremonies are regarded as sacred, handed down through oral tradition only. Many aspects of Native American ceremonies hold only the meaning that they have in the temporal moment. But we have provided you with one take on the Native American elements from Kenneth Meadows' *The Medicine Way* (see the Resources at the end of this book).

	Animal Spirit	Element	Celestial Spirit	Color	Time	Season	Enemy	Manifestation
South	Mouse	Water	Moon	Red	The past	Summer	Fear	Music
West	Grizzly bear	Earth	Earth	Black	Present	Autumn	Powerlessness	Magic
East	Eagle	Fire	Sun	Yellow	Momentary	Spring	Death and old age	Art and writing
North	Buffalo	Air	Stars	White	Future	Winter	Certainty	Philosophy, religion, science

	Animal Spirit	Element	Celestial Spirit	Color	Time	Season	Enemy	Mani-festation
Center	Smoke breath	Ether-void	The cosmos	Blue-green and magenta-violet	Time-lessness	The year	Inertia	Spirit-uality

So you see, in applying the Native American elements to massage, you might quite literally be choosing a new direction: Go northward, my friend. To evoke east/eagle/Fire, a massage therapist practicing Native American techniques might use techniques that activate Fire, using art and writing. Or a massage therapist might use visualizations with Zuni animal fetishes. For instance, the Zuni people believe that the bear represents strength, and the massage therapist may lead the client to visualize himself as taking the form of the bear during the massage session.

Cultural Meld

We are living in a time with a great cultural meld, as these many traditions come together. We see Japanese Reiki techniques being used in lomi lomi Hawaiian massage. We see Reiki techniques being adapted with a Native American twist, as in Ma'heo'o Reiki, developed by practitioner Sheryl Carter. Some practitioners use symbols from Native American culture such as dream catchers, jewelry, medicine wheels, smudge sticks, and ceremonial pipes and fans, all drawing upon Mother Earth energy.

Out of this meld of cultures, one thing holds true as we blend massage approaches to healing: The thread that holds it all together is the intentionality of the healer and healed. This is why our work in these first three chapters has been vital, creating the space within for the proper intentionality to take hold.

One of the key concepts in Japanese Shiatsu massage is to maintain continuity of flow. As you give a massage to your partner, concentrate on keeping your body and mind in concert. Focus on your partner's breathing. The way to do this in Shiatsu is to work from the *hara*. The *hara* is the abdomen and the center of gravity but also the seat of your life force. It is believed to be the origin of ch'i. As you move through the exercises in this book, you will become more fluent in *hara*. It will feel more natural to keep the flow and continuity from your active hand and your support hand. When you do it, your partner will experience the massage touch as just right. The intention, then, is to connect with every touch into the flow of life force energy. This is the magic thread that brings healing to massage.

Part Two

Release Your Body's Life-Force Energy

As we move deeper with massage, we connect with the life force. In passing through the plane of the physical, we have pierced the membrane of the body and the pain it holds. We have reconnected with intuition. The painful information stored in our bodies begins to be released through massage. We become aware of it. Now the mind can become engaged. Mindfulness can be a vital tool in healing. Mindfulness, in and of itself, transforms old patterns into new truth.

Connecting with the flow of life is a magnificent experience. Massage opens us to experiencing that life-force energy, through breath awareness, through the natural rhythms of yin and yang, through colors and auras, through connecting with the elements of nature within us—Water, Air, Fire, and Earth. When connected to the life-force energy, we build trust and safety. After all, when you are connected, you are secure. In this step of the journey, we become like diamonds, hard and glittering.

Chapter 4

Go With the Flow

Think for a moment of the last sunset you experienced—really experienced. Chances are, if you took the time out of your routine to truly watch and listen, you'd remember minute details—the color of the sun deepening as it slid toward the horizon, the shadings of the clouds, the brilliant golden light falling through the trees. Chances are you remember the sound of the wind, the waves on the beach, the shouts of children at play, the scurrying of rabbits or chirps of sparrows. Chances are you stopped to harken to those sounds of life for the very first time that day.

We all know what it's like to be in the flow. It can happen at sunset or it can happen in rush-hour traffic on the freeway. It can happen when we become engrossed in creative work, when we are hiking or running or biking, when we are making love. In that moment, when we are in the flow of life, we are fully present and alive. Our awareness is sharper, clearer. We are energized. We are free from distracting thoughts. We are light.

To be in the flow means to be in alignment with the life force energy of the universe. So much of new age massage is about creating that alignment. To step into alignment with that energy is to let what is most natural take place. It is not about doing or achieving or accomplishing; it is about allowing it to happen.

The River of Life

Pain, old memories, old patterns of behavior, reactivity, anger, fear, sorrow, trapped and unexpressed feelings can all create impediments in the natural energy flow of your body. Massage can release these. Think of this flow of life running through our bodies as a river. Sometimes the current flows effortlessly; sometimes the channel is clogged with debris or we are bouncing off the sharp rocks. The first step is to trust in the flow of the river, to let the river do the work, to propel you.

Empowerment Exercise: River Massage

Put on some mellifluous, flowing music. You may want to choose a New Age tape that features sounds of flowing water, waterfalls, or oceans. The key component of this massage is to set your intentions before beginning. What you want is to experience the flow of energy around and through your body as though a river is flowing through *you*.

Have your partner lie down comfortably. Direct her to take in three deep cleansing breaths. With each new breath, ask her to imagine emptying out a vessel of water within, draining all the old, stagnant water and letting fresh, clear water flood in.

As you massage your partner, you will use long, flowing motions over her body, bringing the energy outside and around you up and down the length of her body. These strokes should be long, slow and deep. You may start with her legs and arms, then work the length of her back. You may start with compressions, rising from the ankle to the thigh. Compressions are deep, gentle pressure.

After compressions, go down and squeeze the feet, one at a time. Stand at the foot of her body. Grip as though you might be pulling a shovel out of the ground. Thumbs are on the sole of the foot; fingers are all on the top of the foot. Squeeze, pulling toes apart; move down, squeezing the ball of the foot. Progress down the foot.

Sweep from the ankle up the leg to the knee. Allow your fingers to curve under the knee. Gently come down with hardly any pressure, back to the ankle.

As you move up and down and around, be conscious of holding the energy in the center of her body, the *hara* we discussed in Chapter 3. Be careful to hold the connection, holding one hand gently against the leg or arm as you move to the next area. Holding the *hara* is vital because you are channeling all the positive benefits of the life force energy back through the body. The massage therapist uses her life force energy to hold the receiver's energy and channel it back. In this way, the massage therapist is a conduit of ch'i.

As you work, direct her to breathe with rhythm of the strokes.

When it is your turn on the massage table, imagine yourself lying on your back floating effortlessly on the surface of a river. Imagine the sunlight falling through the trees, warming your face. Imagine the warm water rippling against your skin. Imagine the gentle pull of the current bobbing you along the surface of the river. Hold in your mind the image of the water caressing your back, moving you along. Hold in your mind for a moment what it feels like to not strive or struggle. Hold it for six deep breaths.

Your task is not to seek for love, but merely to seek and find all of the barriers within yourself that you have built against it.
—From *A Course in Miracles*

The Meridian Connection

Ch'i, the life force energy in Chinese thought, flows through our bodies in channels called meridians. During a new age massage, a trained practitioner such as Erica will use techniques to remove blockages in those meridians. Through intuitive intake, through mini-counseling, and through the sense of her hands moving across the client's body, Erica can identify those blocked areas, working with her touch and the client's breath to release them.

Meridians are connected to each organ of the body, connecting that organ to the life force energy outside the body. For example, imagine your kidneys are feeling tired and depleted. Your kidneys send out that message on their pathways, searching for a store of energy to draw from. Often points along that meridian will be sore if the kidneys are drawing energy from other places in the body. Charts are available to show you the energy meridians and can be found at natural food stores, through acupuncturists or schools of Asian medicine, and through massage schools or on the Internet. For more information, see the Resources at the end of this book.

Empowerment Exercise: Partnered Leg Massage

A great place to experiment with meridians is through a partnered leg massage.

Have your partner lie on his back in a comfortable place. You will want to use massage oil for this exercise. Any kind of cold-press oil will work, but almond or olive oil is best.

We will start with the left leg. Erica often does this to start a circle, moving up clockwise around the body and finishing at the right leg. Start by squeezing the oil into the palm of your hand. Rub your hands together, then allow your hands to glide up the entire length of your partner's leg, starting at the ankle and going to the top of the thigh. Do several long strokes from ankle to thigh.

You are standing perpendicular to his leg, with your belly toward his leg. Now place your hands together above the calf, under the knee, and press down on either side of the shin. Your thumbs are on the outer calf with your fingers on the inner side of the calf. Slide down to his ankle. Keep strength in your hands. You don't want your hands to be soft. Move back up to the knee.

The muscles on the inside of the calf reflex to the liver, while the muscles on the outside of the calf reflex to the bladder. When you move your hands to the back of the calf, you are moving to the muscles that reflex to the kidneys. Imagine a line from the knee to the ankle running down the inside of the leg. Press one finger along this line while placing your hand on your partner's liver. As you do, the liver will heat up, and the points along the liver meridian will become less painful. Have care, because these points can hold a lot of fiery, hot pain.

Now, move to the right leg and do the same.

Once you switch roles, remember as you allow your partner to massage your legs, to breathe with a nice steady in and out breath. Accept any pain that comes up, and breathe through it to release it. As you receive this massage, you may begin to feel waves of exhaustion moving up and out. Keep breathing through the pain and exhaustion until vitality returns.

Energy Centers

In the Hindu tradition, the life force energy is prana. Energy centers in our bodies are chakras, which, as we've learned in previous chapters, are often described as whirling centers of energy and light. Each chakra is aligned on the spine, starting from the root chakra and rising up through the crown. Each chakra vibrates at a different frequency, and each chakra has a color. They are often represented in symbols of many-petaled flowers; you may be familiar with the thousand-petaled lotus of the crown chakra, which represents the attainment of wisdom.

Chakra energy emanates from the body, a life force mandala that is you.

Some see the chakra energies as different expressions of the character of the Divine within us. Think of it as the Divine vibrating at different frequencies, and you are tuning into it as if tuning in to a radio station.

Sometimes we know the Divine as pure love, sometimes as creator, sometimes as power, sometimes as vision.

Let's look more deeply at the essence of each chakra and its meaning.

Root Chakra: Allowance

The movement of the first chakra is slow and dense. It is centered in the body at the base of the spine. Its color is red.

This energy is about purity and security. As purity, this energy represents the moment of birth, when mother and father bring us into the world and we take the first breaths of life. As tiny babies we are innocent, and we are wholly dependent on others for our survival. In the latter respect, the energy is about security: *Will I be taken care of?*

This level is where some of our deepest fears are stored in the body. By working with the root chakra energy, we can uncover our most basic fears; we can understand what we are really afraid of and why.

It is sometimes called "the cradle of the Mother" chakra, meaning it is the source of what we will give birth to in our lives, what we will allow. We can allow ourselves to be truly born, because we can trust that we will be taken care of. We can allow new ideas and ventures to be born in our lives, because we can trust that they will be nurtured and will flourish.

To stimulate flow of energy to the root chakra, massage the feet.

Sexual Chakra: Allegiance

The second chakra is often called the sexual chakra, but that is a misnomer because it is so much more than that. It is centered in the area of the body that contains the reproductive organs, and its color is orange. Its frequency is faster than that of the root chakra.

This chakra represents the energy of allegiance, first to self, then to others. Allegiance to self must come first for the joining with others to be in alignment. Allegiance to self means getting clear about your path. Once clear about who you are and where you are going, decisions about joining with others are clear as well. Should I join with this person or stay away? Is my path here with this person, or is it over there with that other person?

This chakra also represents desire, some of our deepest passions in life, the ones we hold near and dear and may cherish so much we only share them with a select few. When the allegiance chakra is in balance, we can manifest some of our most heartfelt desires in life, whether they are about creating good work or creating good relationships.

To stimulate flow to the sexual chakra, massage the belly in gentle clockwise circles. Strokes should be long and soothing. Or try a soothing backrub to awaken the Kundalini, moving sexual energy up the spine toward the crown chakra.

Solar Plexus Chakra: Will and Power

The third chakra is centered in the belly. Its color is yellow. In Latin, it quite literally means "place of the sun." When you think of this chakra, think of the power of the sun. As an expression of the Divine, this energy is about power and peace.

We think of this energy as the center of empowerment. When this chakra is out of balance, it may be that our idea of power is about conquering and controlling. People who carry extra weight on their bellies are often out of balance with this energy. As this time in humanity, we are coming to terms with redefining power—on the global level as we dialogue about the role of a superpower, on the societal level as we dialogue about the diversity of beliefs and choices in our culture, and on the personal level as we look for new ways of interacting with each other. When our definition of power is out of balance, the place to turn is to empower ourselves. As an individual, this means standing in your truth. So many times we try to control what is outside of ourselves to keep ourselves safe. The shift is to listen to your Higher Self.

When we are in the flow that can be achieved with new age massage, we are lined up with the truth of the Divine within us. We move and speak only in ways that are good for us—and good for the other. It's win-win.

Another way of saying this is that it's about being centered. When you are centered, you are not threatened and you are not reactive. You can listen to the other without defending or fighting back with crushing, cruel words or actions.

To stimulate flow to the solar plexus, practice deep breathing lying on your back, filling up your abdomen with breath. Hold your hand on your belly, at your belly button. As you inhale, push out at the belly, pushing your hand up until you can't take in any more breath. Release.

Heart Chakra: Love

The fourth chakra is centered on the heart. Its color is green. Some believe that from this chakra, the energy of life is distributed to the other major chakras. This is the center of kindness and compassion. Open it up, let it flow, and magnificence will fill your life. It will emanate from you. It will keep expanding.

One way to access this chakra is by tapping your chest with two fingers, right at your sternum while repeating an affirmation such as, "I love all that I see" or "I am surrounded by love." This is like chipping away at the ice that forms over our hearts when we protect ourselves from pain.

Another gentle way is through creating a receptive space in our hearts for love. In massage, meditation, or yoga practice, we can imagine our shoulder blades moving down, cupping our hearts like two loving hands. Move your scapula down your back, lifting your sternum, keeping your spine straight and stable as a foundation of centered, supportive strength. Imagine holding your heart. See how precious it is. It gives you life; it gives you love. Now imagine creating a space within your body enveloping your heart. This space is like an empty bowl within you. Imagine your scapula (shoulder blades) as the two loving hands holding up that bowl. This is the space of receptivity. When we create that space within our hearts, within our bodies, we are welcoming love. And it will come.

Although I may try to write about love, I am rendered helpless. My pen breaks, and the paper slips away at the inevitable place where lover, loving and love are made one.

—Rumi, thirteenth-century Persian poet and mystic

Throat Chakra: Harmony

The fifth chakra is centered on the throat. Its color is blue. This is the place in the body where we can find balance. Its symbol is the lotus with 16 petals. It is the place in our bodies where we can express our emotions and speak our truth. So in many ways, the work on this chakra is about emotional release. We find balance when we bring to a relationship a way of speaking our truth that is not harmful to ourselves or others. If something is out of balance for us in a relationship, we can bring harmony to that relationship by hearing the other out and expressing our true feelings. People who come to Erica for healing work in this area often have sore throats or laryngitis—they have literally lost their voices.

The throat chakra and solar plexus chakra work together. When we express our needs, we gain personal power. When our sense of personal power is in balance, we can clearly express our emotions. To stimulate the throat chakra, use guided meditation during massage to release emotions. Begin massage sessions by stating your intent to release the emotion. Name it. If you are the one giving the massage, check in frequently during the session to ask, "What are you feeling?"

Third Eye: Knowledge

The sixth chakra is located in the forehead between two eyes and about one inch deep. Its color is indigo, and its symbol is the flower of 96 petals, indicating that it spins at a higher frequency. This chakra is the "all-seeing eye," the wisdom of the Divine. Working with this chakra means activating your intuition and trusting it. The energy of this chakra taps into the knowledge of the universe, all knowledge past, present, and future.

The sixth chakra can be activated through gentle fingertip massage all along the brow and the temple.

Crown Chakra: Wisdom

The seventh chakra exemplifies attainment of spiritual wisdom, an all-abiding truth. When this chakra is clear, you can see all of the possibilities. Your perspective is wider, and you see a greater world than this. This is more than your innate wisdom; this is the wisdom of the Divine, the wisdom of the ages. Its color is violet. Think: royal. Think: crown. Violet, as we shall see, is the color of Divine wisdom. The symbol for this chakra is the thousand-petaled lotus. When this chakra is clear and balanced, it draws up the energy from the base of the spine through the other chakras. This is often referred to as Kundalini rising, an awakened energy that comes from the harmonizing of the chakras, producing true enlightenment, spontaneously expressing joy and manifesting love in our lives.

To stimulate the crown chakra, massage the scalp or the feet. Direct your partner through breath visualization similar to the glittering sand exercise we used in Chapter 2.

Empowerment Exercise: Opening the Heart Chakra

This massage is to be enjoyed with a partner with whom you feel truly intimate and safe, because it has an element of romance. You will need some chocolates and sections of sweet oranges. Read on.

To set the stage for this massage session, dim the lights and light the candles. Put on some joyful, soft, heart music. Begin with two hands on the heart, breathing together and holding the image of love coming from your heart through your hands and flowing into your partner's heart. Allow the feelings of safety to build. "I am safe. I am loved. I am all that is good, all that is truth, all that is beautiful."

With one hand on the heart and one hand on the thigh, gently rock your partner's body. Tune in to your heart, your breathing, the music and find the correct rhythm. Now with two hands, do gentle compressions (gripping motions) down your partner's legs to the feet. Squeeze and hold the feet.

Now move back up to your partner's head. Place a small piece of chocolate on your partner's tongue. Move your hands back to his heart. Press your thumb and forefinger gently into points along the top of his shoulder, one at a time, moving from the neck to the outer edge of the shoulder. Now place a tiny section of orange on his tongue. Move back to the heart. Hold for a moment, radiating love through you to your partner.

Move on to the scalp, rubbing with your fingertips. Move all around the head. End with your hands covering his eyes. Hold your hands there, sending warmth and safety.

Now give your partner another piece of chocolate. Hold his ears, again sending warmth and love. End with one hand cupped over his crown chakra, the other hand on his heart. You say, "I am (your name). I am love. I am all that is good, true, and beautiful." Your partner says, "I am (his name). I am love. I am all that is good, true, and beautiful." Now say it together.

Map of the Heart

What is your tendency—to think with your heart or your head? What is your deepest fear? Where is your sense of power? How do you wield power? Do you know your power? How do you forgive? How do you trust? Do you trust too easily at times and not enough at other times? Are you silent sometimes when you shouldn't be? Take a few moments to make some notes in your Empowerment Journal.

Ray of Light: A Chakra Release

Diana (whom we've met in previous chapters) came to Erica at a point when she was ready to start a new relationship, wanting to release old energy from past relationships. As Erica worked the left side of her neck during massage, Diana reported that it felt blue. Erica said it was either her third-eye or expression chakra, and Diana said, "Expression," without hesitating. Erica told her that blue could also represent the Divine Feminine and Mother Energy. Diana reported feeling the energy lift up from her throat, circulating gently above her in a swirling figure eight. Diana reported staying with that sensation and letting the energy flow over her. She said later that it felt safe to express herself because new energy was balancing the intense energy flow.

When Erica moved to the right side of Diana's neck, Diana reported that the whole scene flashed black. When her "vision" came back, it was green. The green flowed down to her heart, then cascaded to her feet. Into Diana's mind popped "lawn": green, safe, soft, the ground. Diana reported the pain in the right side of her neck brought up a memory of painful time in a past relationship. Erica encouraged her to stay with the memory and breathe through it as she continued massaging Diana's neck. Diana reported feeling new energy flow into her heart chakra—green, lush, fertile energy. She asked for that feeling to return to her body, that capacity to love as fearlessly as she did then. She saw the energy flooding in at her heart chakra, then cascading to her feet. She described it later as her desire for that magical lightheaded feeling of love to be grounded. She left the session minus neck pain and feeling that she was prepared for a well-balanced love.

Love is an act of faith, and whoever is of little faith is also of little love.

—Erich Fromm, *The Art of Loving*

71

Your Color Vibrations

Exploring your feelings and sensations around the colors in your life may provide some insight into how your chakras are functioning. If you are like most people, you may have a favorite color you have had all your life. Then again, you may also notice you are drawn to certain colors and may surround yourself with them. Some colors may evoke certain times of your life. When you look back on it, you may wonder, "What was up with that fuchsia phase?" Picasso was not the only one to have a "blue period," you know.

For instance, Carolyn noticed that starting about a month after her divorce was final, she was really drawn to colors such as burgundy, cranberry, orchard red, cinnabar, and pumpkin. These deep, vibrant, sensual colors were colors that she had steered away from most of her life because her mother had always said redheads don't look good in red (Carolyn is a redhead). But all of a sudden, Carolyn was filling up her home and her life with these passionate colors! Red and orange are the colors of the root and sexual chakras, respectively. The root chakra is about survival, about taking care of one's basic needs, about security. As Carolyn filled up her bedroom with a burgundy velvet duvet cover and burgundy silk Chinese pillows and wall hangings, it was about creating security in the most vital place in her house, the bed where she slept and restored herself. The sexual chakra, or orange chakra, is often referred to as the seat-of-the-soul chakra. It is about free-spiritedness, passion, forgiveness, spiritual legacy. It is also about joining, about choosing who we will unite with and who we will not. During this time of her life, Carolyn developed many new friends and partnerships. All of a sudden, this chakra leapt with vibrance. The color was coming back into Carolyn's life after a long time of pulling inward.

Map of the Heart

Take a few moments to note in your Empowerment Journal the colors that make your life. What color is your car? If someone opened your closet, what colors would dominate? What color are your bedroom walls? Your duvet? What color is your kitchen? Your living room sofa? Your shoes? Okay, maybe your car is white now because that's what's practical or it was the last one on the lot. So think instead about the best car you ever had and why it mattered to you. For some it might be that red '68 Mustang convertible or the little yellow Triumph Spitfire.

Touchstone: A Splash of Color

For this exercise, you will need a large canvas. You may want to get a canvas from an art supply store, or if you really want a large area to work on the cheap, get an end roll of newsprint from your local newspaper. These are rolls of paper almost as tall as Carolyn (a petite 5-foot-1), and they are usually available for a dollar or two. You may want to tack your canvas to the wall, or you may find that spreading it across the floor works better.

You'll need paint in all the colors of the rainbow, the colors of the chakras: red, orange, yellow, green, blue, indigo, and violet. The goal is nothing more than play. It doesn't matter what your painting looks like when you are done. It doesn't have to look like something, and it doesn't have to hang in a gallery. You don't have to show it to anyone. The goal here to experience the color. Just get some color and splash it onto the canvas. Swirl it about. Play. Do what you feel. Notice how you feel as you work with each color. Notice how the colors blend together and become new colors. Use brushes of different widths. Use your fingers if you like. The idea here is to get visceral. You are "in" the paint. You *are* the energy. You direct the flow.

Losing Yourself

What is happening in that moment when you lose yourself in an activity? Psychologists call it "cathecting." If it is a canvas you are painting, you and the canvas become one. If it is a path through the woods on your early morning run, you momentarily lose the sensation of your muscles firing and crisp morning air charging through your lungs. You lose the sense of your body.

Marathon runners and triathletes often will speak of breaking through the wall. This is when you are no longer aware of the pull and push of your muscles, the struggle to propel yourself forward. The exertion required to keep yourself running goes unnoticed. It becomes an involuntary action, automatic, seemingly effortless. It happens, too, when we play a musical instrument. A whole generation that has grown up with rock 'n' roll knows well the mesmerizing guitar solo—Eric Clapton, U2's The Edge, or Jimi Hendrix. This is that moment when musician and instrument become one as if united by an electrical current.

The same phenomenon happens in the whirling dance of ecstasy in Sufism. You may know many principles of Sufism through the poetry of Rumi, whose verse is infused with a passion to know love and know the Divine. The spiritual teacher, mystic, and poet lived most of his life in an ecstatic state, living and working in the thirteenth century in a province of Persia that is part of modern-day Turkey. The central principle of Sufism is that love is the way to God. It is believed that human love mirrors that of Divine love. To experience human love is to get a glimpse of the Divine. To fall in love, to lose oneself, is the tool for our consciousness to emerge to the next level.

When you are in the flow, you are there. This is what we mean when we say you must lose yourself to find yourself. What you are losing is not truly yourself; it is the illusion of self. The clinging to that ego-identity of self causes the pain that shows up in your body. It may show up as lower back pain from the fear of change that you have stored in your kidneys. It may manifest as shoulder and neck pain, which can be caused by too much thinking and planning; often your body is signaling that the answer lies in waiting, merely being and seeking the most natural gentle way.

When you lose yourself in an activity that gets you in the flow, you are connected with the flow of life. You have found the truest essence of your existence.

I had a second birth when my soul and my body loved one another and were married.

—Kahlil Gibran, *Sand and Foam*

Auras: Swirls of Color

Auras are the colors of energy that are always with us. They are part of the swirling mists of energies that make up our very being. Auras can be thought of as overflow energies—energies we aren't using—and so that is why some believe they can be seen outside the body.

Auras can signal what is happening in the body. They are an extension of the interplay between your emotions and your physical self, emanating out from your body. Auras can show you if something outside of your personal energy is riding along with you, revealing how you are interacting with it. Once, just after Carolyn's twins were born, she went to a counselor well versed in aura work, and the counselor saw a lot of purple—the color of transmutation—and orange—the color of transformation. The purple signaled that Carolyn had recently transmuted to a new role in life. The orange signaled that big transformations were ahead as she shifted from career to mother, from a managerial position to more creative pursuits.

When we work with auras, the goal is to "make your colors go white." That means you are using all the energies in your body in a complete way. Those who actually see auras have taken a gift they were born with and have not lost it. We may all be born with this ability but have shut down from it, discounting it. Those who can see auras have tuned into it and practiced. To show you what we mean, think of a newborn. A baby doesn't "see" right away. It is believed a baby can only focus about 14 inches away—the distance from breast to mother's face. But if you have looked into the eyes of a newborn, you have probably experienced the way the baby does not focus on your face or look directly into your eyes. The baby may watch above your head, your crown chakra. Cats are another entity that take in and see energies that we are shut down from. By practicing techniques, you can reactivate your senses to take in these energies, and you can learn to see auras.

Empowerment Exercise: Aura Massage

For this massage, we will draw on the same technique of intentionality we used in Chapter 3 in yin/yang massage and in the river massage described at the beginning of this chapter. That is, set your intention to remove the blocks in your awareness to the message of auras. Set your intention to see auras. Declare that you are open to receiving.

Set up your massage area with your partner. Use candles. This will allow your eyes to dilate and receive more light. Set the intention to see colors around your partner's body. Begin by thanking the truth and joy of the Divine for being with you as you open to new experiences. Know that you are protected as you begin this adventure.

Your partner will lie on his back, face up. Place your hands on his solar plexus chakra, or abdomen. This establishes the connection between you. Affirm out loud that you have your partner's permission to explore his aura. When permission is given, breathe together.

Warm your hands with oil. Using gentle swirling motions, spread the oil on your partner's abdomen. As you do so, be conscious that this is therapeutic massage, not sexual. Set aside that energy for another time and place. Work your hands around his belly clockwise. Sweep from the side of the body to the center, then up to the arm. Take one hand and sweep over the sternum and out over the shoulder.

In order to practice "new seeing," don't watch what your hands are doing. Watch the edge of his body, or just beyond the body. Remember, this is about intention. Each time the thought comes in that you can't do this—you can't see an aura—bring yourself back to the place in your mind that says this is possible. Replace the thought with, "I am open."

Afterward, you may want to record some thoughts in your Empowerment Journal.

Channel of Love

As we practice seeking and observing the "who-what-where-when-and-how" causes of blocks to flow, empowerment will flood in. Being in the flow means understanding that we know a certain amount, and affirming to ourselves that we want to understand more. Then by relaxing into flow, we accept that there is a Divine intelligence at work in our lives. It is a choice we make moment by moment, that we are safe to explore ourselves. Perhaps you noticed how many times we spoke about love in this chapter when we spoke about flow, about energy, as though the two are fused. This is no accident. In seeking flow, in seeking to create an alignment with the life force energy of the universe, love is indeed the prize.

Chapter 5

Massaging Breath Awareness

Breathing may seem the most natural thing in the world. Yet this simple tool has the power to transform us in unimaginable ways. The beauty is that breath is with us every moment of every day. Think of it as the secret weapon in your empowerment. Breath is about so much more than relaxation; it is the way to leave behind all the craziness, fear, shame, and pain. It is the guide redirecting us to the present moment. When we pair the discipline of breath with massage, we find we can make quantum leaps in consciousness and vitality.

Breath in massage can be the mechanism that transforms physical and emotional pain into compassion, forgiveness, and grace. It is the way to break through the barriers we set in place inside ourselves. Breath is the place in massage where we can experience the natural high. It is the high that athletes strive for, that lovers ascend to. It is the artificial high that we seek with all of our addictions. But as much as we crave it—natural or artificial—many of us are struck by terror at the thought of it, to be so untethered. Soaring feels good—until we look down.

The breath of empowerment is the way to build a storehouse of safety and security within. The pain has information for us. Through the knowledge we receive from pain, we can integrate our fears. Breath is a vehicle, then, for merging with the pain. It's the way to build inside our bodies a deep foundation of knowledge. Anchored there, in the breath, we can fly high.

[Pain] removes the veil; it plants the flag of truth within the fortress of a rebel soul.
—C. S. Lewis, *The Problem of Pain*

Empowerment Exercise: Let's Go Fly a Kite

The shoulders are a good starting point for working with breath because they often store sharp pain. The shoulders hold a lot of our fear and anxiety about all that we are responsible for. We will direct our focus to the shoulders in various exercises throughout this chapter.

Lie on your back. If it is helpful, you may want to put on some flowing music. You want to direct your meditation as your partner massages your shoulders to the sensation of being a kite soaring, carried by the wind but linked to the earth. You will want to relax, drawing in deep nourishing breaths, letting the vitality flow through you. You and your breath and the flow of life energy around you will merge into one.

Your partner applies oil to his hands. Palms up, he will cup them at the base of your neck. Allow your neck to sink into the palm of his hands. Allow yourself to trust the weight of your head completely to him. Now he slides his hands so that his fingers press into the occipital ridge, at the juncture of head and neck. As the connecting point between head and body, tension always rests here. Breathe deeply six times through it, breathing in through your nose and out through your mouth. As the pain presses into your awareness, release your breath out to soften the pain.

Now your partner slides his hands down your back, underneath your shoulder blades. Allow your shoulder blades to lower to the table or floor. Breathe them back and down, pulling your scapula down your back. Hold this pose for three deep breaths. As you sink into the rhythm of breath and touch, begin imagining yourself as a kite, flitting high above the trees.

Your partner will begin stroking your shoulders. He will start with his fingertips at the base of your head, on the back of the neck right at the base of the ears, moving down the sides of your neck. Then using his thumbs, he will press into the muscle that runs along the base of the neck to the tip of the shoulder. He will alternate pressing his thumb into that muscle, moving out to the tip of the shoulder, then with his whole hand, using long strokes along the same muscle.

As you take in each breath, let it unfurl inside you like the string of a kite unwinding, lifting higher and higher. Feel yourself opening up. As you exhale, feel the air flowing around you as a kite, clouds above and below you. This sinuous, flowing wind is taking you on a magical journey. You are taking in life, vitality, new energy.

As one part of you is flying, another is deepening. It's the difference between lifting off but being disconnected—and soaring safely. This is the role breath plays.

Imagine a tube in your body just in front of the spine, connecting your lower self to your higher self. If you imagine breathing along that tube, as you do, it both expands and shortens, shortening the connection between the lower self and higher self. As it expands, we will feel scar tissue—a tightening or pulling. It's painful as we stir up all that scar tissue. As we keep breathing without judgment and without sinking into our stories, this imaginary tube will pop open and we will be renewed. This is the way scar tissue is released in us. The connection between lower self and higher self becomes stronger.

So you can see there is nothing that you must do. You must not push the pain out. You must not squelch it. All you have to do is breathe. All you have to do is allow—allow the healing power of breath to happen.

There came a time when the risk to remain tight in the bud was more painful than the risk it took to blossom.
—Anaïs Nin, twentieth-century diarist and writer

The Present Moment

Breath is a vital tool for keeping us in the present moment. Direct your consciousness to your breathing, and you can't help but connect with the present and only the present, shutting out all the chatter of your mind, all the past and all the future. What the present can do for you that the past and future cannot is ground you in safety and trust. It can anchor you in rightness, in the hallowed ground of allegiance with the Divine.

When you experience true contentedness in the moment, you know that this moment is all you need. All is provided to you, and you need nothing. All of your future plans are about things that you do not need right now to sustain you; they are only what you *believe* you need in the future to sustain you and may not serve. You are living now. You are alive and full of breath and vitality *now*. Whatever it was in your past that you believe hindered you is not hindering you now. Think of the present as a resting spot, a sanctuary nested deep in contentedness, a refuge from lack or want or need. In this moment, you are completely worthy, and you are completely loved.

Buddhism teaches us that the present moment is all there is. Imagine if you could believe that were really true, if you had no awareness of the past or worries about the future. Imagine how that would color and shape your world. Wouldn't it be dramatically different?

Tibetan sand paintings are intricate works of art that are created over many days. The monks work the brilliantly colored sand in giant patterns spread on the floor of the monastery. They may spend weeks in contemplation as they work. As soon as the sand painting is completed, the monks brush it away. The sand paintings are meant to be only temporal, not to be savored or stored away, because what's important is the process. The contemplative path *is* the goal. Imagine the intensity of joy you would experience if you could know each joy you receive was to be experienced at that moment and could not be stashed away for later. Imagine if you could let yourself experience that fully. Imagine how much you would know and love about yourself if your focus were directed on contemplating your present.

Begin now to cultivate the habit of disengaging from the past and future when you don't need them. Whether the thoughts about your future that lure you out of the present are filled with anxiety or imbued with hope, remember that both are illusory.

Map of the Heart

The image of the heavenly palace is prominent in the imagery of the Tibetan mandala. In this second part of this book, you are moving into the mandala's second concentric circle, the Diamond Circle. This is the place to gather strength and courage. Direct your contemplation as you work to the ways in which you see your own strength. Think of the times in your life you have exhibited great courage. Think about times when that felt like the most natural thing in the world. Think about the times when you felt you needed more courage. Think about the times when you triumphed over a personal challenge. Let these meditations guide you as you contemplate the deepening experience of moving toward the center of your being through the breath. Write about your meditations in your Empowerment Journal.

Sandhya at Sunrise

This Hindu-derived meditation, practiced at dawn, can lay the groundwork for healing breath techniques. By using this tool daily, it will prepare you for greater breath awareness in massage. In Sanskrit, *sandhya* means daily prayer. It only takes about 15 minutes.

Ideally, you will be able to practice this in a regular spot each day. If you have an east-facing view from your window, use that. If it works for you to be outside where you can experience more of sunrise, do that. If you are comfortable going to a park, try that.

Sit comfortably. Breathe deeply, cleansing your mind of all thoughts. Settle into calmness. Breathe in deeply for six full counts.

For this practice, the Hindus read from ancient scriptures. You may choose to use scriptures from a spiritual guide of your choice, or you may collect affirmations and quotes from various sources. Or you may want to use lines of poetry or songs. What's important is that you choose something that resonates for you.

Recite your passage out loud.

Offer thanks to yourself. Offer thanks to all human beings. Offer thanks to the Divine.

You will want to choose a focal point for your meditation, an image or an object that evokes in you the serenity and strength you are seeking. Hindus often use Ganesh, the elephant god who represents the ability to transcend obstacles on the path to wisdom.

Spend five minutes in meditation on your focal point. Use your breath to bring you back into awareness of that focal point. Close with six deep breaths.

Why It Works: Simplicity

The answer to why breath can be so integral to healing in new age massage lies in its simplicity. Each breath is about cleansing and nourishing the body. As you breathe in air, you are bringing oxygen and nutrients to your lungs, infusing your blood with new energy. Your heart pumps that new vitality throughout the body, sending it to your organs, your muscles, your tissue. With each breath, your body is taking inventory of each and every living cell in each and every organ, checking for waste. What is nourishing? What is edifying? What is not? What is not serving the body, the mind, and the spirit? Your blood carries it back to the heart, your center, where it awaits new oxygen, new replenishment from your lungs. All of this occurs in just one breath.

Breath purifies (cleanses), sanctifies (allows us to perceive ourselves as whole), and fortifies (strengthens us for further involvement, action). Breath linked to massage reveals blockages of pain and fear stored in our bodies and helps us to release them and restore the natural flow of our life force. Breath moves to our heart center as a river of life.

Keeping the Bowl Empty: Breath Meditation

One way we can get so off track is in storing too much waste in the body. That waste gets trapped in our muscles and tissues and creates the soreness that sends us to the massage therapist's office.

In this breath meditation exercise, we will begin to create that place inside you for all that is good, all that is nourishing, all that is edifying. This is the first step in relinquishing the fear, craziness, shame, and anxiety that get trapped in our tissues, all those things that a massage therapist such as Erica dislodges in a session.

As you sit comfortably, take in deep breaths. Notice the rise and fall of your breath. Notice its rhythms in your body. Notice the sensations in the room surrounding you. Notice the light and dark. Listen to the ebb and flow of sounds in the room.

Settle into a peaceful, nonreactive state. You need not respond to any light, dark, sound, or sensation. With each breath, let this peacefulness expand in you. Let your active thoughts fall: the "to-do" list, the calendar, the phone calls, the chatter. As you let the emptiness expand in your body with each breath, notice if there are any muscles that release from the constant state of being poised for action. They may spasm or twitch, once freed from the confining state of tensing and stretching, of holding themselves in a state of readiness.

We must let the "action" thoughts settle. Once we do, we can realize that we are living in an open and spacious world, with infinite possibilities. These possibilities do not need to be pursued or attained.

As you let the breaths sink into this new space of emptiness, focus your thoughts on creating a force field around it, protecting this space from action. It cannot be immediately filled with activity. It can just be. Now, the bowl is empty.

Expanding Awareness

Carolyn has had a recurring dream that she is exploring a house, walking down the halls, opening doors and stepping into room after room. Sometimes it is a house she knows well, such as the house she is living in or the house where she grew up; other times, it is a house that came into being in her dream but one that she has been exploring and existing in for the duration of the dream. At some point, after knowing the house well, she comes upon a whole other room, one she didn't know about before. Sometimes it's a whole new wing. The room is usually empty of furniture. It's often brightly colored, painted yellow or blue-sky blue. Often it is filled with sunshine, and the windows are open, curtains are billowing in the breeze. The new open room is quite literally a breath of fresh air for Carolyn's psyche. It is invigorating.

This dream is about that yearning for open space, for a place to expand dreams and hopes, to see new possibilities. When we fill up every empty space in our lives and our psyches, we stop seeing possibilities and feel confined by our thoughts. This shows up in our muscles as soreness. The pain is a signal that we have too much stored up, and it needs to be released.

> The real voyage of discovery consists not in seeking new landscapes, but in having new eyes.
> —Marcel Proust, French novelist

The Stillness Within

The goal of breath in new age massage is to create stillness within that can take you on a magic carpet ride beyond the thinking mind. Most of us honestly do not realize how much of our lives we spend imprisoned in our thoughts. We may not even realize how confining those thoughts are, how conditioned they are by the past.

During a massage, Erica asks the client to focus her awareness on breath throughout. This has the effect of holding back the thinking mind and creating a space for wisdom to flood in. According to Eckhart Tolle, author of *Practicing the Power of Now* and *Stillness Speaks*, wisdom is not the product of thought. He says, "The deep knowing that is wisdom arises from the simple act of giving someone or something your full attention." In this instance, focusing your attention on breath during massage is the first step to creating the space for wisdom to reside in your body, mind, and soul.

In yoga, some of the ancient texts teach that someone who is troubled has more prana, or life force energy, outside the body than within. It is believed if prana cannot find sufficient space to reside in the body, it is because it is being crowded out by stuff that doesn't serve—garbage thoughts and emotions. Breath is the way to influence prana and draw it in so that it flows freely. It is described like this in "Yoga Sutra," the classic Indian text of yoga philosophy, believed to be written in the second century B.C.E.: A farmer who wants to water his terraced fields does not bring buckets of water to each field. He waters the top terrace and opens the retaining wall. If he has laid out his terraces well, nothing blocks the flow of water from the top to the last blade of grass at the bottom. Breath removes blockages in the body; prana follows breath.

Why It's Easier Said Than Done

If breath work is so easy, why must it be taught and practiced? After all, how many times have you heard someone talk about some accomplishment he had aced and say, "It was as easy as breathing."

The reason? Fear. With each conscious breath, we bring up emotions that have been stored in the body because it was too scary to be aware of them. Breath enlivens us, so that we are alive and alert and cannot shut out feelings we have hidden from ourselves. Each breath is a reminder to take in the nourishing oxygen and release the carbon dioxide: Take in the good, release what no longer nourishes. Each breath presents us with the opportunity to stop allowing the fear to reside within us and define our state of being. Learning how to use this magical tool is simply a matter of practice.

Empowerment Exercise: Points of Enlightenment

With your partner lying face up, stand at her head. Press down on the shoulders, using your full hand, alternating one hand, then the other. Ask your partner to exhale through her mouth. With both hands on shoulders, use your thumbs to press points along the top of the shoulder, out to the end. Say, "Breathe in." Do not push during inhales. Remain still as she takes in breath. Then as you say, "Exhale," press her shoulders. It is important to create a rhythm with inhaling/not pressing and exhaling/ pressing. Do not move suddenly; instead attune yourself to your partner's breath and your own breath. Work slowly and deeply.

Inhale, then exhale and press. Inhale, then exhale and press. Repeat this all the way out to the end of the shoulder. Notice which points seem the most painful for your partner. After the first, check with your partner, asking whether the pressure was okay. Was she able to breathe through the pain? Notice if she is gritting her teeth to withstand the pain. That is not the purpose. That indicates there was too much pressure and defeats the point of the exercise.

Repeat this sequence several times, until your partner says she has noticed relief of the pain.

Working With the Pain

While working with breath during massage, it's vital to use the exhale to relax into the pain. And relaxing into the pain is the key to releasing it. As we begin to use breath to guide through pain, it is important to have a shift in how we think of pain. Fighting the pain is like slamming down the lid and locking it tight. Let the pain do its work. Pain is a signal that something is out of balance. Pain is the body's way of moving sadness, fear, and other painful emotions up and out.

Use the following guided meditation to begin to practice changing your reaction to pain. See the pain or fear as your ally instead of your enemy. If we can begin to view pain as a signpost—mere information— then we don't have to struggle so much with it. When ignored, pain expands until we listen to it.

Empowerment Exercise: The Pain Train

This exercise can be done lying down or sitting. Take three deep breaths. Focus on a physical or emotional pain. Feel that pain. Inhale and exhale through your mouth. Be very conscious of your breathing, in and out through you mouth.

Now direct your attention to the pain. Let yourself feel it. Keep breathing. Move more deeply into the pain. Use the breath to be an anchor for your mind, bringing it back. With each exhale, use that movement to settle you physically into the pain. Visualize yourself moving toward the pain. See the pain as a doorway, and you are walking toward it. If you are ready, imagine you are walking through that doorway. Use your breath to guide you. If this feels too much for you, imagine walking up to the doorway. As you move toward the pain with each exhale, ask the pain to speak to you. "Share with me why you are here."

Allow yourself to hold in your mind's eye a receptive place in your body. Continue to breathe and listen. Breathe and move deeper inward. When you receive the answer, you may be tempted to judge it. Imagine yourself standing with your arms and heart open. Muster as much openness as you can. Accept it. When the thought is complete, say, "Thank you."

Breathe for another moment or two. Bring yourself back to your body. When you open your eyes, see that you are safe.

Take a few moments to write in your Empowerment Journal. Just write in a stream of consciousness. Describe the image of understanding that came to you. Describe the words you heard, if it came to you as a spoken message. Write as much as you can about what you understood about the message.

Ray of Light: Shutting Down

Sometimes we simply cannot get past a fear. Erica has been working with a client, Andrew, who is stuck. During a massage, she focuses on moving energy around in his body, and when things begin to happen, when he is relaxing and on the verge of experiencing shifts in understanding, he shuts down.

Erica's assessment is that the fear has risen up in him and taken hold. He cannot see anything beyond it. The fear has activated his ego to protect him from damage or pain by blocking his awareness. The ego will do anything to prevent any reawakening of old pain. The ego says, "We barely survived it the last time. We cannot go here again." When Erica hits this kind of wall with a client, she knows she is in the presence of a major fear.

Andrew has a terror of breathing techniques that Erica suggests. No amount of support or reason on her part can convince him to give it a try. He is certain he will hyperventilate and lose control.

Once she was able to get him to breathe instead of talk, and just as the intensity increased, he quit. He stated that he was absolutely certain he could not go past this point and still live. Erica directed the rest of the session to getting him back into balance. The fear had just begun to move at the point Andrew asked Erica to quit. It left him feeling nauseated for days.

A month or two went by, and the fear and nausea would subside but the pain would build up again and Andrew would return. Each time, Erica focuses on treating only the symptoms. This is the dance a therapist sometimes has to do with a client. Healing massage is not just something the therapist does for you. It is a dance between the courage of the client and the skills of the therapist.

Strength and Power

In yoga, the simple act of assuming the pose of the energy you are trying to summon can be empowering. The role breath plays in yoga is to calm and strengthen the muscles as you assume and hold a pose. The discipline is called pranayama. From Sanskrit, prana translates as life force energy, while yama is "control or mastery of." Breath is used to draw life force energy into the body, modify it, and direct it. Yoga instructors teach that when prana moves, chitta (mental force) moves. This dislodging and releasing of thoughts is what gives yoga its popular moniker of internal massage.

The Warrior pose can give you a sense of subtle strength and serene power. It can give you confidence and presence. One of the benefits of yoga is that with regular practice, you begin to carry your body in a new way. When faced with challenges in your daily life, you begin to respond in your body in ways that are not reactive and do not create more pain.

Touchstone: The Warrior Pose

Stand straight with your feet together at the front of the mat (if you use a mat), feet a hip's width apart. Step back with the right leg into a high lunge. Make sure you keep your left knee balanced over your left ankle (to create a right angle). Square your hips and shoulders to the front. Feel the grounding strength of your abdomen as you establish and hold from this center of gravity.

Extend your arms, palms facing. As you inhale, raise your arms straight over your head. Slide your shoulders down your back, inhale, while pressing your sternum forward. Breathe into the pose. To go deeper, slowly arch back, lifting your gaze to the ceiling. Breathe and hold for six to eight breaths.

To release, inhale and step forward. Repeat with the other leg.

Return to the Hunting Ground: Pushing Your Buttons

Perhaps you don't know what emotions you have stored up inside you, and perhaps you are like Erica's client Andrew, in that every time you get close to them, they seem dark and scary. Perhaps all you know is that your shoulders ache, your fingers are stiff, your back twinges in pain, and your legs are tired.

Situations can build up the pain inside over the years. We can create a storehouse—a veritable silo of pain. We may keep feeding the pain and not even realize we are doing so.

This is where we come back to stalking yourself like a Toltec warrior from Chapter 3. Remember, a warrior is seeking knowledge about the animal he tracks. You are seeking to align with this animal, to understand how he thinks and moves, how he finds sustenance and how he defends himself in the wild. Look back at some of the notes you made in Chapter 1 about how you protect yourself. What are your traps? What makes you vulnerable? If you don't know, think of what can get you to respond when someone is trying to get your goat. Think of how you take criticism. If you are like most people, there are some areas where you can accept the criticism and others where you absolutely cannot. Perhaps there are areas in which you detect criticism when none is intended.

Take a few moments now to make some notes here or in your Empowerment Journal in response to these statements.

On first impression, most people see me as

_____

What I wish people knew about me is

_____

I can be hard to live with because

_____

I would never let anyone call me (examples: unloving/dumb/short-sighted/arrogant) _____

Normally I can hold my temper, but what can really make me ballistic is _____

What really irritates me about (my spouse/my teenager/my father/my mother/my co-workers/my older/younger sibling) is

_____

I wish (my spouse/my teenager/my parents) could be

_____

I don't like people who (examples: curse/are sarcastic/can't keep their opinions to themselves/park on the line/drive too slow/are having a bad hair day/wear dusty shoes/aren't well read/haven't traveled out of the country/leave dishes in the sink/watch reality TV)

_____

When I was a child, I was told I

_____

I wish I _____

If I could be the person I wanted to be, I

_____

Compulsive Thinking

We are sure that if you didn't think you had buttons before, you know you have them now! Those irritations that blow up into anger, those unfulfilled wishes that we didn't even know we had, those judgments we make about others—all of these things can lead to super-charged moments. Or, worse, they can create chronic friction that goes undetected by the observing mind but leads to vague and unfocused feelings of discontent. Your mind can compulsively churn these little things, and it can lead to a storehouse of pain.

Whenever you let these thoughts run without observing them, you are avoiding what is; you do not want to be where you are; you are not in the here and now. On the flip side, when you give too much attention to these thoughts, you are engaging them. The key is to note your thoughts with an observing mind. This is called "watching the thinker." With practice, you will get to the point where you can say to yourself, in the most neutral, calm, and pleasantly entertained way, "Gosh, there is that thought again." During a massage, let breath bring you back to the moment, for this moment is the only place where true contentment can be found. By bringing awareness back to your breath, you are realigning with the energy of prana, with ch'i, with life.

Empowerment Exercise: Alternate-Nostril Breathing

If you are feeling conflict between your mental and emotional energies, this is a good exercise that uses breath to rebalance.

Sit comfortably in a chair or cross-legged on the floor or a pillow. Sit tall, with your back straight and your shoulders relaxed. Rest your hands, palms up, on your thighs. Arrange your right hand so that the forefinger and middle finger are pressing into the palm, with the pinkie, ring finger and thumb extended. This is called the Vishnu Mudra.

Close your eyes as you bring your right hand up to your nose. Close your right nostril with your thumb. Empty your breath through your left nostril. Take a deep, steady breath in through your left nostril, to the count of six. Hold that breath for one count. Press your forefingers on your left nostril, releasing your right. Exhale slow and steady through your right nostril. Exhale slow and steady.

Keeping your forefinger pressed on your left nostril, take in another deep breath through your right nostril to the count of six. Hold that breath for one count. Release your left nostril and press your thumb over your right. Exhale.

Repeat six times.

The Space Between

Breath awareness can be the bridge between emotional reaction and mindful response. Breath awareness training can get you to the point that this seems natural to you. It is the way to hold back the mind, to hold in abeyance the desire to defend or attack. It is the way to take the charge out of super-charged situations in which you perceive your self-image is threatened. It is the way to diffuse the power of the emotion and keep it from overtaking you. When you engage, you "become" the emotion. You act it out. You may think it's not your emotions, but it is your mind at work, thinking, justifying, and supporting with evidence all of your points about why you are right and the other person is wrong. Your mind just got conscripted by your emotions.

But if you take a breath in between those thoughts, you have taken a step toward creating that openness that allows true wisdom to flood in. You take a step back to observing mind. It's not so scary. The threat is not so big.

During a New Age massage, this may happen to you numerous times. An emotion may get triggered through pressure on a certain point. The pain may throw you off track from contentedness and peace. This is where breath can fill the space by allowing pain to move. It can be the bridge that spans from the old way that your body wants to do things and the new way that brings a deep and abiding serenity within. Just one breath opens up that new dimension.

Ray of Light: Erica's Illumination

The first time Erica experienced breath work, it changed her life. It was her epiphany. She experienced moment after moment of illumination and understanding over the two-hour session. As she would breathe through painful thoughts and memories, she just allowed them to be and not react. One of the first illuminations was that she remembered being in her mother's womb and being born. She gained a deep understanding of what her mother felt at the time. She also learned that she carried beliefs about herself that stemmed from her mother's feelings—and she felt incredibly freed when she realized those beliefs were not hers. She quite literally felt the joy move through her body.

Another illumination was about the role of her sister in her life. When Erica was 21, her sister died at age 14. They were close in many ways, and Erica didn't understand her emotions at the time. She was still processing her sister's death 10 years later. Through breath and massage, Erica gained a terrific understanding of who her sister was.

After the session, Erica left thinking she always wanted to be in that alignment, and it set her on the path to do what she is doing today. She went once a week for two years. Breathing through her pain became a life-changing event.

Empowerment Exercise: Victory Through Pain

After focusing on pain during a massage session, Erica often will conclude with sweeping massage movements. Use these techniques for after a session in which one or both of you have worked through a lot of painful areas. This is a very soothing movement.

Rub oil into your hands. Cup both hands together. You are behind your partner's head. Start at the top of your partner's sternum. Start with your hands at the center of her collarbone, where the ribs meet. Move down the center line, down the chest, between the breasts, but not touching the breasts, to the bottom of the rib cage. Move your hands down as far as they can comfortably go. Pull them back up over the chest, in a butterfly stroke, fanning them out over the shoulders, across the top of the arm, around the back of the shoulders to the neck. Let your fingers meet at her neck, on the opposite side of where you started. Turn your fingertips so that they meet. You are cupping the spine. Slide up to the neck, stopping at the occiput. Repeat this once or twice more.

Victorious Breath

As you begin to use new age massage to move the pain up and out of your body, you can turn to yoga breath techniques to celebrate your small victories. This victorious breath exercise can be invigorating, improving your focus and concentration. It is called ujjayi pranayama, or sometimes, ocean-sounding breath, because it sounds like the ocean.

Ideally, you will master ujjayi pranayama by breathing through your nose, but you may start by practicing through your mouth. Sit comfortably on the floor or a pillow with your hands palms up, resting against your thighs. Exhale all the air from your lungs. Contract your throat as you inhale. Some people find it helpful to whisper an "h" sound. Or, think Darth Vader from the *Star Wars* movies. As you inhale in a slow, continuous flow, maintain the contraction in your throat. If you hear a low, hissing sound, you are doing it right. Feel your chest expand. Feel your belly filling up with air. Hold this breath for two seconds. Keep the contraction engaged as you slowly exhale. Repeat for 10 full breaths. Victory is yours!

Every man is a channel through which heaven floweth.

—Ralph Waldo Emerson, nineteenth-century American lecturer, poet, and essayist

The Lightness of Being

Breath by breath, day by day, we begin to know who we really are. We can see that we are not so separate from love. We are not so much less than we desire to be: We are not so heavy. With each breath, we can fill ourselves with the lightness that comes in knowing we are so truly loved and so, so safe.

Each moment draws us closer to a deeper understanding of ourselves and the Divine. Each moment, each breath offers another chance to soften our chattering minds and to attune to a higher call. Every moment, every breath, is a choice, a choice to bring a higher awareness to our thoughts and actions. If we chose to act or think in a way that is not mindful and is hurtful to ourselves or others, we have a chance in the very next moment, with the very next breath, to choose again.

During a massage session, breath nudges the pain, loosening it free. It infuses our bodies with true knowledge and self-awareness, allowing us to heal with love. Breath moves the body back to center, and breath leads us forward.

Chapter 6

Feet, Hands, and Face

The body is more than a house for our physical energies. Now we can see it carries our tender thoughts, our grand dreams, our joy, our sadness, our secret heart desires—as well as our knowledge of the power and wisdom of the Divine. In this respect, then, the body has transformed in our collective thought from house to temple.

In this chapter, we will focus on the benefits of massage to feet, hands, and face. These three areas create the key to unlocking the door to the temple. Each plays a significant role in defining the infrastructure of you—how you are integrated into your body, whether you are comfortable or not, what you are carrying. Each provides a snapshot of the whole. Each represents a vital connection: our feet to the earth, our hands to each other, our faces to heaven.

Working on massage in these areas can create exponential leaps in healing. Because the feet, hands, and face are the opening and closing of the body's energy fields, the body often stores quite a bit of exhaustion there. Energy is going in and out constantly. The hands often are a barometer of acute pain, while foot massage can be the avenue to opening up and releasing chronic pain. The face is the window to authentic expression of our thoughts and emotions. All in all, these three areas hold the clues that will move you to the next level of self-discovery.

Entering the Temple

A cultural mind-shift is taking place in our time. After the Age of Reason, where enlightenment was thought to come to humanity through rational thought and scientific discovery—inspired the Industrial Revolution with its metaphor of the human body as machine—our thinking is returning to more ancient concepts of the body as a vessel for the Divine. One such ancient practice is the Hawaiian tradition of lomi lomi, which blends massage and movement in a sacred form of healing. "Lomi" means "to weave," and the practitioner uses movement and massage to weave light, love, and spirit, and also to unweave stuck patterns in the body, releasing old wounds and antiquated beliefs.

Today, the body is now re-explored in the light of all our current knowledge as an entity interconnected with mind and spirit. Ancient and New Age techniques converge with our most brilliant researcher's quests to understand how mind, body, and spirit live as one. Once again, the human body has become a temple. Meditation, love, touch, and massage can affect this dynamic interconnection. The body as the temple, then, becomes a home for the spiritual energy of true enlightenment.

Think of it. Your body is hallowed ground. It is a wonder of creation. Not only does it contain the miraculous functions of your organs, it holds within it your most illuminated thoughts, your sacred memories, your spirit, your very essence. The body, then, can be thought of as a house in which we worship. It can be thought of as an altar to which we bring our supplication, our desire to summon enlightenment.

The Body as Home

Just as the body is a sacred temple, it is our home. It is where we live day to day. It is vital that this is where we must be more comfortable. Our physical energy can so greatly affect our performance. Maybe you have given a thousand presentations before, but the day that stands out in your mind was the day you were losing your voice. Maybe you planned for months to take a trip to the Greek islands only to find out that you have a strong tendency to get seasick and you spent most of the time losing it over the rail of the ferry. You see what we mean? How you are feeling can *really* dominate your day—and your memories. It's so vital that you feel at home in your body. So many of us don't, with all of the conflicting messages we receive about body image in our culture.

Map of the Heart

Take a few moments to think about how you live in your home—the home that is your body, that is. Are you comfortable? Can you be yourself? How do you carry yourself? Does your stance show that you struggle? Or does it project confidence? Does it show that you are sad? Joyful?

We will draw upon a little feng shui here, the art of channeling ch'i properly in your home space, only we will define home space as your body. When a feng shui expert comes to your home, she will look at whether ch'i flows freely in your house. It must not have any blockages, such as hallways or doorways that are misaligned. Nor must it flow too freely, or you are giving too much energy away. The feng shui expert will note where certain energy, such as family, love, and relationships, is clustered in your house. Are your photos where you can see them? Feng shui experts consider it a plus if you have family photos in a corner that you look at, such as from your bed or your sofa, because it keeps you in touch with your heart. A feng shui expert will also look at the way mirrors and windows are positioned in the house. In your body, your mirrors are your self-image. Ask yourself where you have positioned your mirrors of yourself. What do they reflect back you? What are they *not* reflecting back to you? Sometimes we neglect to reflect back to ourselves our strength and beauty. Your "windows" in your body are your viewpoints. When you look out at your world, what do you see? What data sets are you capturing? What data sets are you failing to collect?

Feet First: The Way Into the Temple

Because the feet provide a picture of chronic pain in the body, massage therapists such as Erica often will start a session by working on the client's feet. It is a good place to start with clients who are tentative about extensive body massage because it has the immediate effect of relieving exhaustion and can build trust. Because the feet are not as intimate, they can be a safe place for clients who have not done much bodywork to grow comfortable with massage.

As with any area of the body that stores chronic pain, there are many layers. Erica often will work with someone over many sessions, incorporating foot massage or sometimes focusing heavily on foot massage, when she senses there are many, many layers of pain to work through. The process is like peeling an onion. A client will work through one layer and reach a level of trust. The trust empowers the client to peel back the next layer.

Foot massage work can then be some of the deepest, most transformational work. Once someone is armed with the courage and commitment, it can be powerful, dislodging years of chronic pain. It takes great faith, but, remember, it only takes a *little* to start.

In the Bible, a reference is made to having the faith of a mustard seed. Jesus teaches his disciples through the parable of the mustard seed about the magnificence that can spring from one tiny seed of faith. He tells the story of a man who sowed a mustard seed in his field. The seed was smaller than all the others, yet when the mustard tree was fully grown, it stood larger than the other flowers and trees in the garden. The faith of a mustard seed can stand firm and tall.

A Buddhist teaching story also tells the tale of a mustard seed. A woman whose only child dies comes to Shakyamuni Buddha, desperately pleading for a miracle to bring her child back to life. The Buddha agrees, but only if she will bring him a mustard seed from a household that has never known death. The woman knocks on thousands of doors in village after village after village, asking, "Have you ever known death?" Quite naturally, the answer is always yes. She hears stories of grief—of old ones passing, of husbands sent to war and felled in battle, of babies like hers who died too young. She listens with care and intent. She knocks on many doors before it dawns on her why she has been sent: She is to discover she is not alone. And then she begins to accept that this is the way of all living things, and her chronic pain and grief ease with enlightened compassion.

Empowerment Exercise: A Single Mustard Seed

In this exercise, done with a partner, you are summoning the intention to create that faith and compassion so that you may do the deepest bodywork you are capable of.

Begin with a foot-washing ceremony. Use a basin or a foot massage tub that you can buy in the home furnishings aisle. Buy some peppermint foot cream, which you may find at a spa or in the health and beauty aids aisle. Peppermint is very soothing and refreshing. You will need towels— the more plush the better. Remember, you are pampering each other.

Fill the tub with warm, sudsy water. Throw in a mustard seed. Not only is the mustard seed a symbol of the faith you are summoning within yourself, it can be a great detoxifier.

As you wash your partner's feet, focus on washing away the old. Your partner should focus on relinquishing and cleansing. When you kneel before your partner, focus on giving. Neither are you slave or master. The reverence of this act of service can open your heart so that you are vulnerable, so that you no longer need to "rule" over what it is you think you need to be in control of. When you are on the receiving end, it can lift you to a place of comfort, trust, and safety. You cannot help but feel honored for who you are. You cannot help but believe that the other sees the Divine in you.

We once read an account written by a young woman about her travels to India. While there, she went to Mother Teresa's mission and asked to volunteer for a time. One of the sisters gratefully welcomed her and, handing the young woman a pair of nail clippers, asked if she could trim the toenails of the poor and needy who had come to the mission for help. This was not the job the young woman expected, and as she walked through the mission she realized that despite her efforts, she could not do it for very long. Far from feeling shame, though, this experience moved the young woman to a deeper realization of basic human worth and dignity and a new compassion for each person's Divine humanity, including her own.

After you and your partner have washed each other's feet, it is time to explore the feet with massage. There are no rules about right or wrong ways to do this. (The only caveat is that if you are working with a woman who is pregnant, you will want to avoid digging into the sides of the heel, which reflect to the uterus.) It may be helpful to acquire a reflexology chart to use as reference. Just explore. Using the chart, use your thumb like an inchworm through the different sections of the feet. Notice where your partner reacts. Combine your partner's breathing with your work. If your partner reacts in pain, tell her to send her breath to that area. Request that she tell you when it releases.

Some may find that they are ticklish when they first use foot massage. Being ticklish is another sign there is tension. If your partner reports her feet are ticklish, switch to slower, deeper movement. Advise her to use the breath to relax. Being ticklish is a sign there is some pain there, and it needs attention.

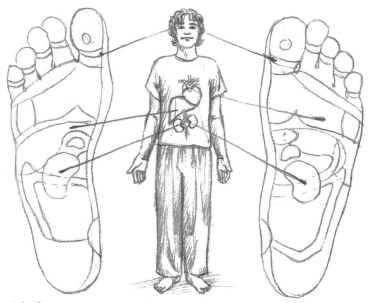

The feet connect energetically to many places in the body. Foot massage helps to release chronic pain.

Ray of Light: Multiple Layers

Sasha came to Erica after being in therapy most of her life for multiple personality disorder. Sasha knew it was important in her overall integration to do bodywork through massage. But she could not tolerate to have Erica touch anywhere on her body but her feet. Sasha reported she felt so much energy coming in through Erica that she could not hold herself together. She was afraid she would dissolve. In some sessions, Erica found she could not even touch Sasha, and she chose to work with energy fields—that is, with techniques borrowed from Reiki and other disciplines.

This can often be the case in people who are very sensitive to other people's energies and the energies of the universe. Even those who do not suffer from a multiple personality disorder can be highly tuned to outside energies. Some high intuitives function well despite being very sensitive because they have a strong, self-contained core. Other high intuitives put up brick walls to protect themselves from other energies, and when in the presence of powerful energies, their walls crumble.

Most of the time, Sasha would allow Erica to work with her feet. Erica worked with her meeting once a week for six months and never worked with more than feet. Sasha's energy was very fine. Like a satellite dish, Sasha picked up signals on all levels—physical, emotional, and spiritual. In Sasha's case, she had no strong central core to keep all of her energy integrated and the energy that was not hers distinct. Working with Sasha's feet in such an intense, focused way made Sasha give herself much-needed support and helped her to feel more stable in a profound and lasting way.

People usually consider walking on water or in thin air a miracle. But I think the real miracle is not to walk either on water or in thin air, but to walk on earth. Every day we are engaged in a miracle which we don't even recognize: a blue sky, white clouds, green leaves, the black, curious eyes of a child—our own two eyes. All is a miracle.
—Thich Nhat Hanh, Buddhist teacher

Being Grounded

Your feet are your connection between heaven and Earth. The Earth, too, is a temple, and body is an extension of Earth as temple. Feet are the conduit between the earth as temple, and the way the body becomes a temple. Your feet, and your stance on Earth, can make you feel less diffuse—more in your body and your awareness of your body and its place on Earth. Your feet can help you bring your emotional and spiritual energy into your body, into your realm. In other words, you are not all over the place.

A spiritual teacher once told Erica, "It's time to come down into your toes." Most of the time we are not fully into our bodies. When we are in reactive mode, just responding to external influences, we are in a constant state of readiness to run, to fly away. We don't want this experience. We don't want to see it. We don't want to hear it. We don't want to be still. "Coming down into your toes" means fully being in your body. It's a profound experience to realize we have so much more space in our bodies than we knew. That is why working with foot massage can help us feel stronger and more integrated.

Empowerment Exercise: Tree Meditation

Stand with your feet lightly planted on the earth. Ideally, you will be able to do this outside, where you can be barefoot with the soles of your feet touching soil or grass. It can, however, work inside with your bare feet on carpet.

With your knees slightly bent, focus on the warmth in the soles of your feet. Feel the vitality of the earth, its energy vibrating against the soles of your feet. As you breathe, direct your focus to the breath moving in and out. Envision roots moving down from your body and taking hold in the earth. Feel those roots stretch and unfurl into the ground beneath you. Stretch tall, extending your torso, your neck, your legs. Take in the expansion. Envision the earth's energy rising through the roots up into your body. Feel its warmth, vitality, power, and sustenance fill you. Really let yourself feel the sustenance as it rises through your body—your torso, your shoulder, your neck. Let it rise through your head, then burst out like branches of a tree. Stretch taller, connecting to the vitality of the sky. Now you are linked to heaven and Earth, and you are expanded.

Stay in this meditation exercise for another few minutes. This stance has a strong yin/yang rhythm to it, and if you take a few more deep breaths, you can bring your focus to that rhythm. Focus on the energy coming down from heaven (yang), through your head, through your spine, through your sacrum, down to your feet and to the earth (yin). As the energy reaches the earth, feel it rise again through your feet, your sacrum, your spine, your crown, to the sky. Let yourself breathe through at least six cycles. Feel how calming the rhythm of this energy can be.

Bones of the Earth

Another way to ground yourself is the Bones of the Earth massage, a hot-stone massage technique that draws upon the Native American tradition and is very popular at many spas, resorts, and massage therapy centers in the Southwest. As Taos-based Bones practitioner Chris Sherwood puts it, "with stones in hand, we will follow the whispers and allow the merging of our hearts, through the relationship of our hands, the stones, and the body of another." The massage is intended to help you reconnect with Mother Earth. The rubbing of the hot stones on your body can create deep listening—to ancient voices, to deep within, to the Earth.

Vertical vs. Horizontal Expansion

When you experienced the link between earth and heaven through your body, did you feel expanded? Wasn't that a magnificent feeling? That expansion in your body is the same energy that has brought humans over the course of history to build great cathedrals and monuments in homage to the heavens. In many cultures, many times, people have worked together to gather the materials of the earth to create these vast, magnificent spaces. Think of the dome of St. Peter's, the vaulted ceiling of a Gothic cathedral, the stones of Stonehenge, the pyramids of Egypt, the ancient Zapotec city of Monte Alban in Oaxaca, Mexico.

It is believed that the vertical movement of energy is the energy of the Divine. God moves up and down, from heaven to earth to sky and through us. It is our job to bring that energy of the Divine through ourselves and send it out horizontally into the world. That is our purpose. That is why we turn to massage to clear out our bodies of toxins, illness, pain, and trauma, so that we remain clear enough to receive the "rain," the vertical energy, of the Divine and we may act, moving that energy out into the world.

Hands-On Learning

Hands are an extension of the heart. They are the way we extend the energy of God (the God of our individual understanding) to others. Hands are the way we connect with each other and the way we work in the world. For that reason, they are pivotal.

Like the feet, the hands provide a picture of what is happening in the body, and reflexology illuminates that picture. The hands, though, show us where the acute pain resides. That is why often people who receive hand massages report to Erica that they feel instant relief.

Hands connect intimately with heart energy and hold our immediate, acute aches and pains.

Empowerment Exercise: Heart Topography

Blindfolded, take your partner's hand and explore it with your fingertips. Notice the different textures of his skin. Notice where it is rough and where it is smooth. How do his hands feel? Are they bony, fleshy, soft? Explore, sometimes laying your palm flat against his, sometimes spooning your palm over the back of his hand. Explore, gripping his fingers and sliding out to his fingertips. Hold his thumb back, hyperextending, then fold it back to the palm of his hand. Press your thumb into the mounds of flesh at the base of each finger. Press the nail beds. Trace your fingertips across his heart line and lifeline on his palm.

When you meet anyone, remember it is a holy encounter. As you see him you will see yourself. As you treat him you will treat yourself. As you think of him you will think of yourself. Never forget this, for in him you will find yourself or lose yourself.

—From *A Course in Miracles*

Your Heart Work

Meditate upon your heart work in the world. In what ways do you give your heart? How do you help people? Think of your community volunteer work or your involvement in church activities. But go beyond that. What kind of friend are you? If someone made *It's a Wonderful Life* about you, what difference would you have made? Why are *you* uniquely qualified to do this kind of work? What qualities exist in your personality and in your belief system that guide you?

Massaging the hands can bring great comfort because it can relieve acute pain. Massaging the fingertips can relieve headaches because the fingertips connect (in reflexology) to the head and sinuses. Much of the flow of energy from the hands leads directly to the heart, so a hand massage can open up the heart chakra. To focus on the heart, massage the pads of the fingers, swooping across the band of skin to the thumb. This directly opens up flow to the heart. Bringing immediate relief can build trust between client and massage therapist.

Why is opening energy flow to the heart crucial? Not only does it bring immediate relief, it begins to dissipate some of the negative energy stored in the body, flooding the body with good blood flow and unblocking obstructions. It gets the circulation moving. It gets the pain in motion.

In Balance

The body is always looking for a point of balance. It will do this in whatever way possible. Some of the ways it chooses to achieve balance are some of the ways that build up pain in the body and send us to the massage therapist. Over time, layers and layers of pain can build up in the body. The longer they go unaddressed, the deeper the pain will go in the body.

One of the reasons Erica does a lot of work with hand and foot massage is because these are often the places where the body begins to open up that first layer of pain. As an example, if your lungs are continually congested and you don't deal with it, over time it becomes asthma. If you don't deal with it at that level, the body sends out the pain through the body's meridians, or energy channels, associated with the organ under stress or in pain. The body will keep doing this, because no matter where the original pain is, it must send the pain to the furthest place from the heart. Always, the body protects the heart from pain because if the heart suffers trauma, the whole body suffers great trauma. This is the body's built-in high security system. It must always protect the heart. So its job, when it has no other way to release pain or trauma, is to push the trauma away from the heart. That is why pain often it ends up in the feet and hands.

> Your crown has been bought and paid for. All you must do is put it on your head.
>
> —James Baldwin, African American writer

The Face of You

Our facial muscles can hold a lot of pain because this is the place where we are vulnerable. The face is our opening to the world. It is something we feel we have to guard. We learn very early in life not to "wear our heart on our sleeve," and we tamp down too much expression in our faces. We walk around with "poker faces," disguising our true emotions from people we are unsure of. This may become a habit when we are in a business or professional setting, and we may carry it over into our personal lives, sometimes shutting out our loved ones from our true feelings. But when this no longer is a struggle, when it is no longer vital to hide who we truly are, the self comes back into the body. The light comes back into our eyes. It is okay to radiate. You are in your power.

One of the primary benefits of facial massage, of course, is release from acute pain. We store a lot of physical pain in our faces. Our foreheads and eyebrows move up and down, crinkle and curl, expressing the full range of our emotions. Over time, some of the expressions we most commonly display become etched on our faces, giving credence to when your mother told you your face might freeze that way. When you have a cold, your sinus cavities can collect a lot of goop and gunk, clogging you up and leaving you exhausted. You can also store a lot of pain in your jaw line. You may not even realize what you are doing with your jaw line (clenching?) throughout the day when you are frustrated or tired. But your jaw knows.

Empowerment Exercise: Dropping the Mask

This exercise will help you shed the mask you wear for a new look. Have your partner lie on his back—ideally, elevated on a table. You will sit behind him.

Place your left hand over his left eye, your right hand over his right eye, slightly cupped. There is not much pressure here. This is gentle. Notice that your thumbs rest quite naturally between his eyebrows. Draw your thumbs up, across the eyebrows and out, over the temples and out to the ears. Press little points along his eyebrows, always moving out. Press points along his sinus cavities, moving out. Press along his jaw line, starting from the chin and working up to his ear. When you reach his ear, loop over the top of it, pressing with your fingertips back behind the ear to the base. Swoop your fingers over one more time, as though you are sweeping hair behind the ear.

When that feels complete, move into a scalp massage. Press all four fingers against the scalp, moving in circular motion, starting from the hairline and moving to the back of the head.

You will want to use light pressure and smooth, sweeping motions. All of the muscles in the face and scalp are small, and your goal is to stir them up. After you get that energy flowing, you will find your eyes will be clearer. You will see better and hear better.

Now, switch places. As you receive your face and scalp massage, focus your breath and your awareness on shedding your mask.

If you want a more active exercise, you may want to visualize some statements or say them aloud. "I am a business person. I don't have to be a business person right now." "I am a parent. I don't have to be a parent right now." "I am a strong person. I don't have to be invincible right now." Mentally go through your many masks. Shed them one by one.

Your Essential Question

Each of us carries in us one big question. It may originate from a pivotal event in your childhood. It may come from a message you received early in life, and thereafter you had a doubt about yourself. An essential question can be something like, "Am I worthy?" "Will I be betrayed?" "Can I trust you?" "What can I learn from you?"

Whatever your essential question is, you carry it on your face. You carry it in the way you stand, the way you move your body. It's a question you generally hide from the world. But the truth is, it's there every moment of every day, in every personal interaction. It lies there in our faces before we assemble them into our public masks. Sometimes, when we drop the veil from our public masks and others catch us, they may reflect to us worry we didn't know was showing.

The essential question is the place your thoughts go when you drop down out of the "to-do list" chatter of the day. It's there when you first encounter someone. It follows you in all endeavors. It forms the structure of your frame of reference—how you compose and organize your thoughts. What might that one big question be for *you*?

The Sacrum: Where Fear Resides

Out of the 206 bones in the adult body, 19 are in our hands and 19 are in our feet. The bones in our face are delicate, particularly along the jawline, where many people suffer pain. Our bones define the structure of our bodies—the structure of the temple. They define its shape, and they determine the body's strength. In the case of our faces, our bone structure defines its character.

Feet, hands, and face—each plays a role in defining how your body sits on your sacrum, how you are structured. The way you stand on your feet is determined by your sacrum. Your sacrum, or your pelvis, is the foundation of your body. The sacrum can be the place in your body that some of your most visceral fears reside—about survival, about sexuality, about allegiance, about safety, about trust. This is the center in the body of the root and sexual chakras. Because they reside there, they affect your stance.

To understand the energy you store in your sacrum, examine your sexual history. Would you say your alliances have been enriching? Meaningful? Problematic? Demeaning? Would you say you have made some bad choices? Would you say you can express yourself freely in a sexual relationship? Are there some ways that you do, but are there other ways you hold back? In what ways do you see yourself as a sexual person? Are you sensual? Are you passionate? Are you wild or tame? Are you aggressive or passive? Would you rather stand naked in front of a stranger or a longtime love? Would you rather be naked with someone than have to get real and let someone know your authentic self?

Map of the Heart

Take a few moments to write in your Empowerment Journal about your deepest fears. What threatens your sense of survival? Think of statements that someone dear to you has made that cut the deepest. Why was the criticism so scary? Why did it hurt so deep? Why did it make you fight and claw back with angry words? Why did it terrify you that this person saw you this way? Think about the ways that you trust or don't trust people. In what areas is it easy to trust, and what presents the greatest challenge for you? Think of the people you feel safe with. Contrast them with others that may enliven you or terrify you. Think of the people you steer clear of and why.

Empowerment Exercise: The Path In

To relieve lower back pain and loosen the sacrum, start at the feet, working with the hands and moving up to the head. Working at the feet, give special attention to the soft spot of the foot, in the arch, just below the toepad. This area reflexes to the kidneys, where exhaustion is stored, and can start to open up chronic lower back pain. Working at the hands, you may be able to bring immediate relief to acute pain. As you "finish" each finger, lift your partner's arm, pulling on the finger, extending the arm. This stimulates blood flow to the heart. Working at the head, hold your thumbs above his forehead for at least 30 seconds, breathing deeply. Gently place your pinkies at his ear. Follow with your ring finger on his scalp, then your middle finger, then your forefinger. Finally, place your thumbs gently on his forehead. Hold it there until you feel him relax into it. This can draw energy up from the root and sexual chakras into the crown, relieving exhaustion and pain stored in the lower back.

Mission Control: The Body's Communication System

The feet are vital to the body in motion; they reflect the stability of your sacrum foundation. Both feet and hands contain within them a constant state of readiness to flee or to fight. Because of that, they can hold a lot of pain that we might not even realize is there. We use our feet and hands without a lot of gratitude for what they do. As a therapist, Erica is often astonished that people are still walking around. To accomplish movement efficiently, the feet must maintain an overall background of muscular tone. Tone comes from regularly giving relief from all the standing, walking, and running we do; too much of any one of these, without enough rest, makes for tired muscles and taut ligaments. So, too, with our hands. We do so much with our hands, many of us working on computers for much of the working day.

Touchstone: Give Me the Spread

The bones and ligaments in the feet and hands are necessary for them to function as they do—bending, twisting, rotating, flexing and so on. The ligaments, when overused, become tight, like rubber bands frozen in place. Those bones and ligaments can hold a lot of pain.

This exercise widens the bones of the feet. A modification of this can be used for the hands. With your partner sitting, kneel in front of her. Grasp the top of her foot in your hand. Now lean the weight of your body into her foot. As you do this, she should focus her breath and her awareness on widening her foot. You, too, will want to focus on deep, cleansing breaths to focus. As you feel the bones and ligaments in your partner's foot soften, take a deep breath and increase the pressure, leaning more of your weight into her foot. Do this until it feels complete. Then release. By pulling the ligaments slightly apart, we can release a lot of built-up tension.

Holy Rhythms: Craniosacral Work

Craniosacral work is one of Erica's favorite techniques to use because it can be so effective and transformational. It can be done anywhere on the body, but often Erica will start at the head. Craniosacral work focuses on the natural rhythms of the brain and spinal cord to achieve alignment. That's why it can do so much work to loosen up the sacrum and realign our stance. It can open up tight areas and draw energy up through the spine and out. A layer of fluid surrounds the brain and spinal cord. The skull and vertebrae float in this fluid. It flows around the brain, through the brain stem, through the spinal cord, to the sacrum and back up. It's like an ocean, constantly moving. Those who work with craniosacral therapy and truly believe in it often refer to craniosacral fluid as condensed Holy Spirit. They believe that the flow in our bodies is a level at which a deep connection is made to the Divine.

Restoring the Flow

Some think of the craniosacral fluid as a recording of our life experience, as though it is quite literally written in our bodies. When there is a trauma, the fluid records it on a physical level. Little dams get built up. The flow of the nervous system doesn't send impulses all the way down to the fingertips. Something is stuck, and the flow gets ragged.

Massage therapists often employ craniosacral work when someone has experienced a trauma such as an auto accident or severe sports injury. They can often sense the blockage of craniosacral flow from cradling a client's head in the palms of their hands, holding it near the occiput, the base of the head where it meets the neck.

The goal of craniosacral work is unblocking all the dammed-up places. Erica thinks of it as the deepest level at which a massage therapist can touch the human body. During craniosacral sessions, people tend to get very relaxed, sinking into a near-sleep state. As the dams come unblocked, people can feel parts of their bodies twitching, jerking, and opening up.

To receive craniosacral work feels like being in a cradle. It is very gentle, very loving. It is often done with the client lying on the table and the therapist at the client's head, cradling his head in her hands. Another modality has the therapist sitting up on the massage table behind the client as he sits up. The client leans back on the therapist, and the therapist gently cradles him with her body. She moves his arms, legs, head, and neck from that position.

Ray of Light: Replay

Jennifer came to Erica not quite a year after a devastating auto accident. Jennifer was eight or nine months pregnant at the time of the accident. The first session, Erica used basic massage with a little craniosacral work.

The next two sessions, Jennifer brought her newborn baby, and Erica did exclusively craniosacral work. The baby would lie next to Jennifer on the table, on her tummy. At one point, when Jennifer had sunk into a very relaxed state, her arm jerked up. She instinctively put the other hand out to protect the baby. With her one hand she was grappling with a steering wheel. It was like watching a film in reverse.

Once Jennifer's body replayed the trauma, it was as if all of the emotional underpinning had been released. Jennifer's stuck emotions were like pins holding the physical trauma in place, creating the blockages in her craniosacral flow. Replaying the event was like erasing the recording. After that session, Jennifer reported relief from pain and stiffness.

From Seeking to Knowing

The search we have been on—for your true core—has brought you closer to knowing. This knowing is storing up in your body, exercise by exercise, massage by massage. The deep knowing will bring you to a point of alignment with your highest intentions. Using massage to get the face, feet, hands, and body into alignment is not just a matter of muscles, ligaments, bones, and fluid. Once you know alignment, you will begin to feel when something is not right and you can bring yourself back. Once you know alignment, you are ready to enter the temple of mind, body, and spirit harmony and enlightenment.

With each chapter, you gain more tools to practice this transformation. It comes through prayer or meditation. It comes from cultivating stillness within. It comes from looking within for ancient, lingering pain. Massage stimulates the pain to rise to our consciousness. Massage gives us the capacity to release it from our faces, our feet, our hands, our bodies. Now it is time to step forward from knowing to empowerment.

Part Three

Connect With Your Deepest Spirituality

And now we encounter the test. It often happens when we embark on healing work with massage: We hit a dark passage. This is a sign that you are moving ever deeper still. The third layer represents the emotional plane. In using massage to tap into your deepest feelings and your most painful wounds, you may meet many challenges. These may be the rooms of the palace of the soul that you had sealed off from yourself. Ahead, we turn to some of the most visceral ways to work through it—through getting in touch with your senses, through using movement and meditation. This is where you begin to trust—and release. This is where you make the decision to reclaim your heart and your soul and the joy of your body. This is where the torch begins to burn more brightly.

Chapter 7

Relax, Trust, and Release

It takes great courage to commit to self-discovery and the work of mastering empowerment. Sometimes the journey leads you to walk through fire. If you have picked up this book, you have come already equipped for the fire walk. You have the commitment and the courage. You have the deep flame of desire for your life to be transformed. You are willing to submit your throbbing, aching body and your old ideas about yourself to the heat that will render a spiritual alchemy. You already know deep inside yourself that the metal will turn to gold.

In the series of exercises in this chapter, we will walk with you through the fire. We will guide you in building a stronghold of safety within, a deep, unshakeable trust in new truth. We will guide you in releasing and working through layers of fear, and we will help you gear up again when the going gets rough. These techniques will lead you forward to a healing that you want more than the pain and fear you know. This is the fire that purifies; it will not consume you. It will transform.

The Fire Walk

The fire walk symbolizes the shift from allowing a painful past and a frenetic present to shape your life to moving toward a new, peaceful reality defined by your inner self. When you come through the fire of emotions and feelings your body releases through massage, you are realigned, restored. You walk differently, you sit differently. You are free of pain and vibrating with truth. You are comfortable in your own skin.

The fire walk is usually not just one massage that brings on a catharsis and is resolved. Oh, that it would be so simple! The fire walk is a process of relaxing into massage, trusting that it will lead you to higher ground—and releasing. Over time, you begin to see the new, brighter place ahead. This light leads you forward. It beckons you so that you come to want something more than the fear and the pain you know. The hot coals are beneath your feet, but you know you want to get to the other side. And so you gear up again to take the next steps. And you find you are stronger and more equipped than you were before you started across.

> That fire (of fear) does consume, but grace bestows upon us a titanium personality structure invincible enough to withstand the heat.
> —Marianne Williamson, spiritual teacher and author

Ellen and Scott are two of Erica's success stories, and we will follow them through this chapter. In truth, every client who comes to Erica is a success story. Every time someone submits to the emotional and physical transformation of healing massage, there are little surrenders, little openings. The healing does not always take place in one huge cathartic moment, with trumpets blaring. More often, the miracles come in tiny steps.

Ray of Light: The Light Ahead

Ellen has not yet made it all the way across the bed of hot coals. But she has committed to a long journey because she sees that what she wants has been offered to her. She has been involved with a man off and on for a few years—a man Erica feels is Ellen's soulmate. Ellen is using bodywork with Erica to work through the blocks she has in understanding the relationship, which has had many gut-wrenching ups and downs. When Erica listens to Ellen talk about this man, she hears that despite the pain and doubt, he is Ellen's other. The Universe wants this for them. This is something they can have.

Ellen's most primal fear is in her belly—her solar plexus, her power source. Through massage, Erica works with Ellen to access her power source. That's why when Ellen experiences a transformational massage, she gets nauseated. Ellen has lived most of her life with an injury that was discounted in her family. No one believed her, so she has just lived with it silently. That's what she had to do to survive in her family, and that's what she knows how to do well. The incident from her family of origin drove the pain deeper and tighter into the center of her body.

Because Ellen gets nauseated and sometimes throws up after her massage sessions with Erica, she has rigid beliefs about how she should breathe. She declines to experiment with new breath techniques and resists Erica's instructions, certain she will be sick if she complies. Ellen is not yet willing to change her rules. Still, it's her overarching desire to unite with this man that keeps Ellen coming back, even through the challenges the sessions present. Over the years that Erica has worked with Ellen, she has educated herself and found a high-paying job. Erica describes Ellen as brilliant and self-sufficient.

So Ellen is moving toward the life she desires. When she is doing the body work, she is always feeling better. When she has long periods of away time, the ice begins to freeze over her body. But when she is engaged and she comes every week to two weeks, her fingers, arms, head, and neck feel better. She is not so prone to panic attacks. Ellen's fire walk is one of using the heat to melt the "ice" that overtakes her body, the fear that holds her back from the life she truly wants.

Safety and Trust

The key to getting to the point of transformational release of pain through massage is to create your own safety. You must experience a trust that you can be safe no matter what is going on around you. You cannot achieve complete trust when your safety depends on ideal circumstances. Yes, it is vital that you know without a doubt that when you reveal, you will be heard. Yes, it is vital to know that whatever you might reveal to another (your massage partner) will not be used against you. You will not be judged. You will not be attacked. You will not be seen as weak. You will be accepted as you are.

But true, lasting, and abiding safety is based on inner perception. If we wait for it to come from the outside, we will never truly feel safe. That's why the fire walk works. You are telling yourself as you walk on hot coals that you are walking on a cool, soft bed of grass. The mastery of the fire walk is the ability to completely focus your attention and create the reality you want. During massage, when you feel physical pain releasing in your body as your massage partner works with you, some of the best tools for holding you in that magical spell that gets you across the hot coals are the breath techniques we used in Chapter 5.

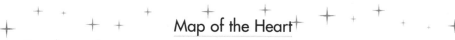

Map of the Heart

Together with your massage partner, take some time to write in your Empowerment Journal about your fears. Who or what has hurt you the deepest? What is the worst thing that has ever happened to you and why? What feels unresolved for you? What are you still searching for? Have you had a taste of it? Did a dream slip through your fingers? Have you loved and lost? Take a few moments to share with your partner about what you wrote in your journals. It is vital that you have this exchange. You must trust your massage partner enough to be able to share past traumas and bring them forward. Together with your partner, resolve to begin healing work on these issues.

Together, you and your partner should agree on how you will work through the massage sessions in this chapter. You agree to acknowledge your past pain. You agree to commit to healing that pain, and your partner agrees to support you in that. You agree that if it is uncomfortable for either one of you, you will ask to stop and the other will honor that. You agree that any sharing stays between you and is not to be shared with anyone else. You agree that what is shared is received without judgment.

Finally, before each session with your partner, call upon the light and power of the God of your understanding. Ask for protection.

Layers of Fear

There are times, of course, when we do experience release in a place or with a person, and it's not safe. It is vital that we acknowledge that in the past, we may have opened up to someone when it wasn't safe, and it may have left some damage. We may react by committing to ourselves *only* to open up when it is safe, denying ourselves the opportunity to cultivate new skills for creating safety. When we have created our own inner safety—the portable kind that goes everywhere we go and functions even under stressful conditions—then we know we are safe all the time.

When we find ourselves in present-day situations we perceive to be unsafe, the feelings often stem from childhood traumas. As a child, our only job is to survive. If a child feels threatened, his immediate fear is survival. So many of our fears stem from that child's need for survival and security, and those fears are stored deeply in the root chakra, located at the base of the spine. This is the part of the body that is the most protected. As a result, it's also the most difficult to unlock. When a lot of pain is stored there, it is beneath many, many layers.

It takes a commitment to a series of massages to work through this type of deep, stored pain. You may start by focusing on the head, neck, and shoulders, the places where most people store their most immediate pain. Or you may focus on head, feet, and face because all those places are external. It takes time to build up the trust to do deeper work in the lower four chakras—the heart, solar plexus, sexual, and root chakras.

Starting with the intention to work through the layers of limitations in your body, have your massage partner do a series of massage strokes working through the lower chakras. Use these suggestions, but be spontaneous and let what is happening in the massage guide you and your partner in spending more time in one area or another. Begin working in the heart chakra area, in the shoulders, sternum, and upper back. Move underneath the sternum, to the belly button area, working the solar plexus chakra. Below the belly button, move into the sexual chakra, swirling a hand clockwise on the belly. Moving down into the legs will start to open up both the sexual and root chakras. Then as you lie on your back, your partner slides a hand up your back to the kidneys and back up to the shoulder blades. Your partner will balance the bodywork in the lower part of the body by closing at the head or working at the neck.

Eckhart Tolle, author of *Practicing the Power of Now* and *The Stillness Within*, encourages us to envision our accumulated pain as an entity, something that occupies space in our bodies and minds. He calls it the "pain-body." Indeed, it can feel as though another entity inhabits us—there is so much pain residing there.

Massage moves through layers of stored fear to illuminate chakra energy on the path of the fire walk.

Ray of Light: Two People

It's as if two people inhabit the body of Scott. Scott is constantly moving. His hips squirm. He often pops his neck. He often has intense pain in his neck, head, and jaw. It's like he is sitting in a boiling hot cauldron of his own body.

And it *is* as if Scott is on fire. In his profession, he often fights mightily for the underdog. Erica senses in his body a fury at the injustices to his clients. It stems from his pain of being abused as a child by his father. Scott's passion for his cause of protecting others from injustice is the fire that cleanses and heals. But because his journey across the hot coals is not complete, the fire within sometimes burns in a way that doesn't completely release his anger and pain. Through focused body work with Erica over time, Scott can channel that fire into a purifying fire.

Ray of Light: Original Pain

Ellen comes to Erica because her hands are crippled by pain. She experiences intense neck, head, and shoulder pain. The nerves to her hands are blocked, and her hands freeze up. She has lost some strength in her hands over time.

Ellen has manifested many things in her life that illustrate her growing competence—an advanced degree, a lucrative career, and a beautiful house— through the time she has worked with Erica. She is going longer and longer periods of time with less pain. But she is still struggling with the relationship in her life. She knows the more she takes on during a massage session, the closer she can get to manifesting the peace she desires.

Empowerment Exercise: Comfort Massage

Because some of our deepest fears go to survival, a massage that gets to the pain in the root chakra can be volatile. This massage offers a safe way to experience the primal fear that often resides there. Erica finds this is a part of the body where people "do not rest well." She will notice if someone feels particularly vulnerable in the root chakra area by observing the way he or she moves or sits. An example of not feeling comfortable in your skin is if you aren't comfortable sitting on the floor or curling up in a chair. If when you sit, your legs are closed most of the time—that is, crossed or pressed together—you may be protecting yourself from these stored-up fears.

This soothing backrub starts with you lying on your tummy. Your massage partner will rub warm oil on your back, starting at your legs, using long, deep strokes up the buttocks and over the whole back. Then she'll move to the gluteal muscles in your buttocks. She will make a fist and place it on your buttocks, turn the fist about a quarter turn and press in, using alternating hands. This massage is called commonly called the mashed potatoes massage. It stirs things up yet it feels good.

A warrior considers himself already dead, so there is nothing to lose. The worst has already happened to him, therefore he's clear and calm; judging him by his acts or by his words, one would never suspect that he has witnessed everything.

—Carlos Castaneda, twentieth-century mystic and Toltec warrior

Confronting Big Fears

When a fear comes up (in life and during massage sessions!), it's huge. That's fear's job. It must make itself very large if it is going to stop you. Most fears when they come up seem life-threatening, *feel* life-threatening ... that's what it feels like on the gut level.

How does the fire-walk warrior proceed? It's not that there *is no fear.* You must acknowledge the *strength* of the fear. Part of that fear exists to protect you. The primal fear is that you will lose your life—lose your self. But the fear has a vital message for you: The fear is telling you how much you hold your life dear. You *want* to live. You *want* that passion for life. You *want* your life to be vibrant. You *know* there is more, and you reach for vitality. That's the strength of your fear, and when you channel that strong energy, it's a tremendous positive force. You state, *"It is my intention to live through this fear."* At that point, you are ready to do what you were sent to do. You can move through the circumstances surrounding you with complete trust that you will create that safe reality. You say, *"I am the master of myself."*

Empowerment Exercise: More Than This Fear

You must remember you are more than this fear. There is more of you than there is of the fear. The more of you is stronger and mightier than this fear.

Your massage partner will start off with a massage at the head, then move with you into these affirmations. Your partner's goal is the shake up the head. He will rub his fingers over your head, squeeze your shoulders, slide one hand under the flat of the shoulder blade (you are on your back), lay the flat of his other hand on your shoulder, and shake the shoulder, and shake and shake it. As the receiving partner, you breathe in fast exhales, pumping the diaphragm, with strong outward expulsions.

Afterward, list with your partner some of your fears. Know that all fears spring from one or two core fears. When you list them, you may see how they are all connected to one root fear. Look back over your journal at the massages, meditations, and visualizations you have noted while working on the many exercises in this book. Which fears come up most commonly? Is there a core fear?

I am afraid _____.

Now say: "*I am bigger than this fear.*"

Your partner says, using your name, "_____, you are bigger than this fear."

You repeat, "*I am bigger than this fear.*"

Repeat as many times as necessary, increasing the volume each time. Let your voices get bigger than this fear as well.

> When you come to the edge of all the light you have, and must take a step into the darkness of the unknown, believe that one of two things will happen. Either there will be something solid for you to stand on—or you will be taught how to fly.
> —Patrick Overton, educator, poet, and playwright

Self-Discovery: It Can't Be Used Against You

Remember that release in any form is absolutely acceptable. The Universe abhors a vacuum. What flows in after a true letting go is love. There is no more place for fear.

When you enter into the level of the deepest work, it may seem like everything you once knew and could stand on with certainty is crumbling to the ground. This may seem like the most desperate of times. It may seem like it only gets scarier. Too much is being taken away from you. "No, no, not this," you may say. Some of these feelings are your old stories about yourself being stripped away. You have used them so long to protect yourself you don't know how you can live without them. Hear us: You won't be in need of this old pain and emotion and fear. You can survive without it. You will *thrive* without it.

Empowerment Exercise: Safe Release of Trauma

Many people store their deepest pain in their hips and thighs. It is the deepest darkest pain because we store in the pelvis, in the thighs, in our sexual organs, some of the things we consider to be most negative about ourselves. Those things tend to be more volatile for us. This is where people store the stuff they most want to keep hidden. (Not surprisingly, from themselves as well as from others!)

In the following Shiatsu massage exercise, you will work along the iliotibial band (IT band), which runs on the outer thigh from the knee to the hip. This massage cannot be done on the floor. If you have bought a massage table, use that; if not, use a sofa or bed. Your partner will stand on your left side with his left hand on your thigh at the knee and his right hand on your left abdomen. All these points along the IT band reflect to the colon, which is the center of emotion in the body. Think gut reaction. Think butterflies in the stomach. This is the place in our bodies where we start to feel sick if we push ourselves past the place where we are comfortable.

With his left hand, your partner will gently press on points from the knee up to the thigh while holding his right hand on your belly above the colon. Your partner will do this until he starts to feel warmth in his right hand. Your partner will urge you to keep breathing through any pain. If you report the pain is too sharp, your partner will take his pressure back one notch. You may sense some places along the IT band have excruciating pain. Your partner will keep going slowly back and forth over those places until he feels warmth and feels them beginning to relax.

To take this exercise one step further, your partner will press his belly to the massage table on the left side. He will lift your knee up and cradle it against his chest. Notice your knee is against his heart. This stance brings in gentleness and conveys trust and safety.

Your partner continues on to gently press on points along the inner thigh as he did on the outer thigh, almost like pressing fingers on a clarinet. These points will likely be more volatile than those on the outer thigh. For women, this could be more emotional than for men. Your partner will go from the knee to the groin as far as it feels comfortable to go, and he will direct you to exhale each time he presses. Your partner will say to you, "I am holding you." This conveys the message from his heart: *Yes, this is painful. Yes, this is difficult. I am with you. I am helping you. You are not alone.*

To end the session, your partner will take the palm of his hand and press from the knee up toward the groin, using warm, gentle presses. Stop just before reaching the groin. It's important that both partners feel comfortable with the touch.

Primal Scream

A good primal scream is fabulous for emotional and physical release. It can make significant progress in releasing deep root chakra pain. The deeper in the body it (the scream *and* the pain ...) comes from, the better. Try incorporating primal screams into a massage session like the one in the previous section, and notice the release you have. If you are not scream-ing deep enough—if you are screaming from your throat or your head—you'll notice the pitch is too high and your throat will get sore. Strive for a full, rich, deep tone. Let it swell from your body. Let it resonate.

Stepping Off the Cliff

Sometimes clients who come to Erica will experience a release through their arms and hands called tetany. Tetany is a release that produces a tingling sensation all through the hands and arms. Sometimes the hands will cramp up. Sometimes people have contortions and can't stop. What is happening is that the body is dumping pain and dumping it fast. The mind is struggling against that. The mind says, "Oh no, something is out of control." It tries to pull back all of the energy rushing out of the body, and that produces the trembling and tingling.

This release can be terrifying when it happens, and if you struggle against it, the experience can be painful. Clients often report pain in the tiny muscles of the hands. The fingers sometimes become hyperextended, or sometimes fold up like a blossom. The way to deal with the release of tetany, when it happens, is to acknowledge that fear is present and drop into the release. Relax into the experience. Do not allow the fear to suck you up. It takes incredible courage to go through such a powerful unfold-ing. But it's like a woman giving birth to a baby; there's no other way but to go through it.

During massage, when someone reaches a cathartic moment, Erica's role drops way back. The client "takes it" at that point. There may be tears, rage, or a coughing fit. There may be outbursts. The person may scream. The person may pound fists on the table or kick her heels or stamp his feet. Some clients have thrown up. If you are administering one of the massage exercises in this chapter and your partner comes to this point of catharsis, be willing to step aside and let the response hap-pen. Give your partner the freedom and room to express *everything*. If you are the receiving partner, *let go and know you are safe; your partner is there with you.*

Ray of Light: Subtle Shifts

Sometimes the turning point is subtle. In the case of Scott, Erica focused on craniosacral work. It's like Erica and Scott are slowly moving through ice. This is the point in the firewalk when the fire begins to cleanse, to melt through all the layers of fear. She focused on craniosacral work in his head because she sensed places in Scott where a powerful, cleansing internal fire resided, one that would not rage in him like a bonfire—that "on fire" feeling she senses in him. Craniosacral work, she believed, was the key to unlocking the most powerful places in Scott that lay frozen deep within. She compares his skull to the continents of a frozen Earth, jammed against each other. Over time, she is bringing flexibility to his head. During the craniosacral sessions, she will "wash" energy from Scott's head down his spine to the rest of his body.

Scott is very guarded in his body. When he came in after experiencing a nonstop low-grade cold that lingered for a month, Erica took it as a good sign that Scott was softening all over. Normally, his style would have been to attack the cold, to crusade against it. His shift was in seeing the cold as part of the process. He was exhausted. He had big bags under his eyes, and his kidneys and adrenals were stressed. Exhaustion is often a signal that the body is beginning to relax into what you're really feeling. Scott is a very mind-over-matter person, so this was a subtle but significant shift. Exhaustion from having all that drive and passion for 20, 30, or 40 years covers up all the feelings you won't allow yourself to have. But Scott was opening up to it. He told Erica he was no longer grinding his teeth.

There is a crack in everything. That's how the light gets in.
—Leonard Cohen, Canadian songwriter

How Did It Serve?

The greatest shift of all comes when you ask yourself the question of how the harm, the stored pain and difficult emotions, may have served you. What did you learn? How can you put that learning to good use?

This release moves you into an easy, empowered stance, and it is a key step on the path of mastering empowerment in mind, body, and spirit.

Once you can begin to see how these traumas served you and how your body held them for you (often for many, many years until you had the strength to release the pain), you can see how you can forgive the traumas you have experienced. You can even thank them. Express gratitude if not for the harm, then the valued outcome. Express gratitude that you have busted out of a paradigm that may have otherwise remained coiled intact within your deepest self. Express gratitude that you sought answers that would never have sprung from your body if not for the pain.

Touchstone: Gratitude

Begin with a discussion with your massage partner. Sitting on the floor, the one who has just experienced release is enfolded in the other, her back against his chest, so that you are cupped together. Express compassion for your body, the pain it has held there. Say a prayer of gratitude for its release. When expressing your gratitude, allow it to come up in any form. There may be more tears. You may want the calm of silence. You may just want to sigh, or sleep. Some of it may be pure joy, and you may not want to stop talking about it. Let it be as it is.

The healing energy of release and trust.

Follow this with a soothing back massage, with the receiving partner on her tummy. Use warm oil, and spread it up and down her body. Use long, soothing strokes; avoid any trigger point touch. Do the strokes with warmth and softness.

Gearing Up Again

When you embark on the fire walk there inevitably comes a time when you question whether the journey is worth it. The pain may be too intense. It may be too difficult—or uncertain—to flip back into your regular life between massages. You may look back on the months leading up to this moment, and you may wonder if all the havoc is someday going to pay off.

It's natural to hit a moment of doubt. To continue with the metaphor of the fire walk, it's like a break in concentration. You can be walking across hot coals, and you are training your mind not to let the heat stop you from crossing over. And then, all of a sudden, your mind screams, "Danger! Danger! There's fire here!" But this is the fire that does not burn. It does not consume you.

If this kind of obstacle comes up during a massage session, the way back, as we acknowledged earlier, is instantaneous—it's through breath. Notice that your thoughts have taken over. Do three deep breaths with long exhales. Outside of a session, you can use the following steps to get yourself back to the courage and commitment you require.

Every warrior returns home from battle to nurse his wounds and heal. As before there was a time for stalking the truth, now is a time for the warrior to recount battles and champion his strategy in achieving victory. For your fire walk to healing through massage, now you must make time to take stock of how far you have come.

On a deeper level, when you experience doubt between massage sessions, on some level you are not accepting that the journey is painful. *"Must I suffer?"* you ask. "Must I suffer *this much?*" It's perfectly natural to question in this way, to momentarily lose sight of the role suffering plays in bringing us to healing. Without pain, we do not know humility. Without suffering, we do not learn compassion for ourselves or others. Suffering cracks the shell of the ego. It can get us to the point where we no longer can keep up the game that everything is okay. *"It's not okay that my body hurts this way. It's not okay that I have to live with this every day."* Or even, *"It's not okay that I am doing this alone."* And then ... you marshal the forces of energetic healing. You begin to move toward divine enlightenment.

By not accepting any longer the way you used to do things, you turn to new resources—in yourself or others. You see your path in a whole new way. You see that you don't have to suffer; you only have to ask what it is you must learn next. This is what Eckhart Tolle means when he says, "Suffering is necessary until you realize it is unnecessary." As you practice transforming your stored pain into enlightenment, you will grow less patient with the doubt and the suffering. You will see the way to bliss, and you will no longer be willing to turn back. Instead, you say, "Okay, time for a quest. What do I need to learn from this?"

There is no need for suffering. God is here.
—Rumi, thirteenth-century Persian poet and mystic

Empowerment Exercise: The Well

This massage exercise can be the well to which you return to replenish yourself. It's the water that cools the hot coals so that you can keep moving forward. Before this massage, take time with your partner to recount some of your victories.

In this exercise, the receiving partner is lying on the table. The massaging partner places his left hand on the top of his partner's head, at the crown. We will want to establish contact between the crown chakra and each of the other chakras, working up from the root chakra. First place the right hand on his pubic bone. Rock him slowly, deeply, with an even flow. Then the massaging partner holds her hand still, feeling the energy connection between the left and right hands. Next she will move up through the sexual chakra (hand on lower abdomen), power chakra (upper abdomen) and heart chakra, rocking each time, then holding it still. At the throat chakra, the massaging partner holds her hand an inch above the throat until she feels warmth, connection, tingling under her hand. Repeat on the forehead at the third eye, then the crown.

To conclude, the massaging partner will lift her left hand off the crown, making a fist, pointing her thumb toward the crown chakra. With her right hand, she will make a fist, pointing her thumb at the root chakra. Imagine the chakra energy spiraling from the right thumb up your partner's body to the left thumb. Breathe together and feel the energy flow.

When a situation has been dedicated wholly to truth, peace is inevitable.
—From *A Course in Miracles*

Your New Truth

The way ahead is through truth. When you hit self-doubt about the fire walk, the truth is the light that will reach out to you and draw you forward. Massage by massage, you uncover the truth, revealing it layer by layer. You eventually come to a point where you can see a clear, final truth. In other words, the pain is finite. When you are working through pain in your body and releasing emotional pain, know that only so much is stored in your body. It may seem limitless because the pain intensifies with each layer, but it is not. There is an end.

When you reach the point of clear vision, you will realize you have already started a storehouse of truth within your body. Your body will know that it doesn't have to react and think in the same ways. It's a way of feeling that can't be described in your mind. It's like the feeling you have when you smell bread baking; you are immediately transported to a place that is nurturing and wholesome. This sense, this place, this feeling, is individual to each person. For some the place of change is in their stomachs; for others, in their hearts. You only find the way it feels in your body as you emerge through the fire walk. Once you find your place and know it, safety and strength is always there. You don't have to respond to outside influences, feeling like you are at their mercy. You can calmly observe. You can step in to your power. You can say, "I am the one who decides what my life looks like. I am the one who decides how my body, my mind, and my spirit will respond."

How do you know what you feel is the truth? You know it *in your body*. You don't store the truth so much as you vibrate with it. When you store pain, you are heavy. When you are filled with truth, you are light. At this point you will move from seeker to knower, from discoverer to practitioner. You no longer stalk, you quest, you lead, with joy.

Be a warrior; shut off your internal dialogue; make your inventory and then throw it away. The new seers make accurate inventories and then laugh at them. Without the inventory, the assemblage point becomes free.

—Don Juan Matus, from Carlos Castaneda's *The Fire From Within*

Ray of Light: The New Scott

In one recent session, Erica did a lot of work in Scott's forehead. The forehead has the energy of knowledge, and the massage worked to undo the energy of past knowledge. For Scott, what has been the truth to this moment is no longer the truth. It means going out into the world he has created based on that knowledge and seeing the truth in a whole new way.

Just after this massage, Scott had a big event ahead in his work life, the arena that has served him so well, channeling his crusading energy. He was learning, though, to come from a different place, not as the avenger, yet he needed to summon his resources together to continue to be successful and function in his professional world. This was new territory. He had accepted the abuse from his father and the allowing his mother did. This meant playing a different role as crusader and truth-seeker, as someone who is infused with truth, and with empathy. It meant facing his own fears that he would be like his father and examining his fears of intimacy and power. This new way of being was playing out on all fronts of Scott's life.

He had to be able to allow himself to feel the changes in his body, yet still be functional. When you are doing the fire walk, one of the struggles is flipping back and forth between your old body and your new body. You must allow yourself to be in process.

Empowerment Exercise: Deep and Subtle

A practitioner of craniosacral therapy works in the place within the body where thought is held in place by emotion. To begin experimenting with craniosacral work, have your partner lie on his back. Hold his head in the palms of your hands. Both of you rest into this. Hold it until both of you feel connected and at ease. Be sure both of you can breathe easily and naturally.

Once relaxed, place one hand on his forehead, the other cupping his occiput. Again, rest into this position. Relax down into yourself. Feel your breath and pulse settle. Move your focus to your partner. Allow yourself to feel his pulse and his breath. Sink into them, below all the physical action of the body. This is the level where the craniosacral pulse resides.

Let your hands copy the movement coming from the depth of your partner. You will feel your hands moving toward each other, then away. This is the craniosacral pulse, or flow. The bones of the body float in this ocean of fluid. You will be able to feel the ebb and flow of this ocean's tide. Once you have established this feeling in your hands, hold your hands in the "together" position, the place where they are closest together at the back of the head. As you hold it, you will feel pressure building in the pulse of your hands as the craniosacral fluid builds up. Hold against the pressure for about 30 seconds, then release. You will feel a moment when the craniosacral fluid is perfectly still. Then it will flow again. Your partner's breathing may deepen. He may even slip into sleep. This is good.

The head is the easiest way to begin learning about craniosacral therapy, but you can feel the flow wherever you touch the body. Remember not to hold for longer than three minutes. This is too deep of a hold to maintain for longer than that.

Moving Toward Joy

The moment of empowerment is when you are totally willing for the door of release, healing, and joy to be opened for you. You have no more resistance. You trust that the new world is there—that it will be there when you seek it. Empowerment in action is a total thrill. It's fun. What you're experiencing is the joy, no matter what is happening. What you are seeing and feeling is the joy—the joy of understanding, of illumination, of release. Everything you see is through the eyes of joy. Life should be this high all the time!

You learn to make decisions based on faith that whatever you need will come. That faith springs out of knowing, something that you have proven to yourself that you know to be truth. It arises from the word of God (as you understand God to be) revealed in the body's voice, the sacred communication between you, your partner, and the restored flow of Divine energy that comes when you experience transformational massage. The deeper you listen, the more is there, the more trust you have. Joy multiplies and unfolds like the opening petals of the lotus blossom.

If you cannot accept anything on faith, you are doomed to live a life dominated by doubt.

—Kris Kringle, in *Miracle on 34th Street*

Empowerment Exercise: The Burning Bowl

Remember your list of fears from earlier in this chapter? Take them and write them one by one on slips of paper. Together with your partner, drop them one by one into a large bowl. Do not share them aloud. Do not speak of them. Write each one and silently drop it into the bowl. The silence says you are done with this. You do not even need to talk about it any more.

Now, light a match and burn these slips of paper. Let them go up in flames. Your fears are consumed, yet you survive. You are whole. You are healed.

Afterward, try this joyful, loving partnered massage. It embraces a newfound exploration of who you are in body, mind, spirit, and soul. Sitting cross-legged on the floor across from each other, start with one partner reaching out her right hand. She strokes the receiving partner's arm all the way up to his shoulder, kneading the shoulder, then moving back down the arm and forearm, massaging the fingers. Then exchange roles, working the right side. Now switch to the left side. Exchange.

You shall be free indeed when your days are not without care nor your nights without a want and a grief, / But rather when these things girdle your life and yet you rise above them naked and unbound.

—Kahlil Gibran, "Freedom," from *The Prophet*

Empowerment Exercise: No Brakes On

From this point forward, you are ready to take on massage in a whole new way. Take some of the exercises you have done so far with this book—only now you can do them with no brakes on. If when you practiced breathing in Chapter 5, you held back because you were afraid you would hyperventilate, don't hold back. If the foot massage in Chapter 6 was surprisingly painful, go back to that. This time, let your partner increase the pressure. Have her stay a little longer on a pressure point.

Breathe through it. If your partner is working on your head and you feel it start to tingle, go into it. Say, *"I want more."* Go into whatever your experience is, so it can be magnified.

Peace Is Every Step

At this point, you have now uncovered the information you need. You have completed an apprenticeship of the self. You are now empowered. You are ready to put what you know about yourself into action. You are no longer stalking knowledge about yourself. You are no longer a student. You are a master. As Buddhist teacher Thich Nhat Hahn teaches: *Peace is every step*. You move ahead in joy. You see with new eyes, the flame of enlightenment that does not burn but illuminates and heals.

Chapter 8

Hear, Feel, Taste, See, Smell

To see is to know. To smell is to remember. To hear is to harken.
The five senses make us feel more alive. Hearing a bell …
tasting chocolate … catching a scent on the breeze that reminds
you of childhood—all of these things expand your experience
of living and breathing. They increase your vibration. You
begin to operate at a higher frequency.

Heightening your senses is like boosting the RAM on your
computer. Suddenly your whole system functions better and
faster. You wonder how you ever did without it. No more
watching the hourglass, the ticking watch, or (for Mac lovers)
the spinning beach ball. Your computer gets you there and
gets you there faster. When you operate at a higher frequency,
with more voltage and a clearer, more expanded vision, you
experience more enlightenment. Think of it as the broadband
way to healing.

Mastering empowerment means having at the ready many
ways to put it into action. That can only come with practice.
Over time, you will cultivate and feel at ease with the many
techniques to activate your sense of empowerment, and using
them will deepen and enhance your experience of New Age

massage. When you rehearse them, when you play with them, when you become facile with them, they become second nature. They become part of who you are.

Just Play!

A teacher once said to Erica, "We would all be much better off to use the word play instead of work." Sometimes we are so serious about life that we forget to have fun. It's not just at the office that we are at work. We even work at having fun. Carolyn had a friend who once said, "Never be in a hurry to have fun." It is a personal gut-check to notice when you are in a dither to get gathered up and out of the house to go have fun somewhere else.

We even work at healing ourselves. It's not work; it's a journey. When we look back on the journey of becoming more empowered and more enlightened, undoubtedly we will remember the joy even through the struggles. In fact, the joy is heightened by the reward of breaking through the struggle. So it can all be fun. It's not a drudge. It's not mundane. It shouldn't be a pain. It's exciting. It's a magical mystery tour.

Whenever we forget this, our five senses can lead us back. That playfulness can help us remember how alive we can be. So just play. There's no parent, no teacher, no editor, no inspector, no boss. No one is saying you can't. No one is saying it has to be a certain way. There is no right or wrong.

Play keeps us vital and alive. It gives us an enthusiasm for life that is irreplaceable. Without it, life just doesn't taste good.
—Lucia Capacchione, author and art therapist

Empowerment Exercise: Touchy Feely

You may remember when you were a child a party game—often played at Halloween—in which you reached into a black box. Inside were different objects: spaghetti for brains, hard-boiled eggs for eyeballs, that sort of thing. Your black box need not be so spooky. What we'd like for you to do is start with a box. It may be a special box that holds some significance for you: a little wooden chest with brass hardware, a hand-painted wooden hinged box lined with velvet. You will fill it with items that you love to touch. That could be a square of plush velvet, a scrap of tatted lace, a marble or smooth stone, a crunchy red maple leaf, a long chiffon scarf embroidered with gold thread, a squishy ball or block of yellow clay. (Remember Boo Radley's box in Harper Lee's classic novel, *To Kill a Mockingbird?*) Gather your items over a week or so.

Schedule time on a weekend morning to go through the box and its contents. Play with the items. Don't just touch them with your fingertips. Feel what it's like to smooth it over your cheek. Or lie on your back and place the item on your forehead—or your belly. Wrap the scarf around your neck and dance around the room. Tie it a hundred different ways. Dip your fingers in water and smooth it over the clay. Remember, no one is watching. Be silly.

The second part of this exercise is to meet with your partner for this book, who should also have filled a box with items. Blindfolded, you will each go through each other's boxes. Explore the objects. (Hope your partner didn't revert to third-grade-Halloween-carnival mode and put cold spaghetti and hard-boiled eggs in the box. But even if she did, get in touch with the spirit of the moment and enjoy it!) There is something about being blindfolded and touching something that can heighten your sense of touch. Did you notice that? Bring this awareness of the surprise and delight of touch to your next massage session.

Make a Joyful Noise

Sometimes Erica urges clients to make noise—any kind of noise—during a massage. Sometimes she will cue them to make noise by chanting or toning or grunting. Sometimes she will direct a client simply to hold his mouth open. The jaw is the strongest joint in the body. Erica guesses that nine tenths of the people she treats have TMJ (temporomandibular joint) disorders, such as jaws that click (count Carolyn in that group!) or pain in jaws and temples. All these occur because of holding tension in the jaw. Some people find it very challenging to breathe in and out of the mouth or even just to exhale through the mouth, but doing so can really relax the jaw.

Erica finds that many clients don't want to make a sound during massage. Women especially resist making noise because they have been conditioned not to be loud. Men don't because they are uncomfortable with others hearing them. During sessions, she encourages people to grunt, scream, sigh—whatever. Afterward she may assign them to go to the foot of the La Luz trail, which is a trail on the eastern edge of Albuquerque in the foothills of the Sandia Mountains. The trail climbs to the Sandia Crest (elevation: 10,678 feet). At the trailhead, sitting in the foothills, you can look out at the city and the valley of the Rio Grande. She tells people to make big sounds—big, big sounds that will roll out through the foothills and the valley. Their assignment is to make a big enough sound to fill up the foothills, the city, the valley, the volcanoes at the western edge of the city, Mount Taylor in the distance and beyond to Phoenix, some several hundred miles away.

> The larger loneliness of our lives evolves from our unwillingness to spend ourselves, stir ourselves.
> —Carol Shields, author of the Pulitzer prize–winning novel, *The Stone Diaries*

Empowerment Exercise: Shout to the Hills

Assign yourself the task right now of shouting to the hills. Remember Maria in *The Sound of Music?* The movie opens with the camera swooping across an alpine meadow to Julie Andrews twirling atop a mountain, spreading her arms and belting out the lyrics of the song. And remember what they say about Maria back at the convent? "How do you solve a problem like Maria?" goes the song. "How do you catch a cloud and pin it down?" This is your chance to be a problem. Fill the hills with your sound. Let someone else figure out what to do with you.

Playing—with no thought to the result or no concern about the reaction of others—is the key to expanding our awareness. It gets us out of the box. There aren't any rules. Notice what your body feels like when you play. Notice what it feels like when there are no rules, when no one is saying it has to be done this way and done by this time, when no one is saying you can't do it. Do you feel soft all over? Do you feel like jelly?

Mastering Mindfulness

Tapping into your five senses can be one of the quickest ways to cultivate mindfulness. Mindfulness is the state of being acutely aware in a panoramic way of all that is around you in the present moment. When we are rushing around, reacting to whatever is right in front of our faces, we are out of mindfulness. When we are only paying attention to what's on fire, we lose sight of the deeper embers burning within. That state of mindfulness is the ability to see what is happening right here, right now. It arises from cultivating stillness and harnessing the full range of our senses—sight, hearing, tasting, smelling, and touching. It arises from being conscious of the ways in which we are interacting with others. And the way to be conscious of how we are conducting ourselves is to pay attention to our thoughts and the way we hold our bodies. Notice if you are grinding your teeth or furrowing your brow. Notice the next time what it feels like when you release it. Notice what thoughts came in that made you tense up, and notice what thoughts allow you to relax.

With practice, you can train your mind to drop these obstacles.

Let's take a moment to look at some of the obstacles to mindfulness. Within each pairing, we have brought in its opposite. It is so much easier to replace an old habit of reactivity with a new habit that is empowering. It's the difference between saying, "Don't do that," which requires an act of will to squelch a perfectly normal impulse to control or envy or resent. Instead, recognize the unwanted thoughts. Note that they came up. Acknowledge them. Don't push them out, nor engage them. Move forward to the thoughts of what you want to bring forth within yourself. Envision it. Write lines of dialogue for yourself. Rehearse them.

Controlling vs. Observing

So much of the pain we cause ourselves arises from believing we can control things we cannot control. If you are not exactly sure about what we mean, you may never have been married or been a parent. Do one of those two things, or both, and we assure you, your control issues *will* come up. As Carolyn often says after a long afternoon trying to get her two little people (four-year-old boy/girl twins) to nap, "It comes down to this: Free will. You absolutely cannot make another person eat or sleep if he or she does not want to."

In *The Seven Habits of Highly Effective People,* Stephen R. Covey distinguishes from your Circle of Influence and your Circle of Concern. He depicts these as concentric circles, with the Circle of Influence as the smaller circle within the Circle of Concern. The Circle of Influence is what you can directly influence. Beyond its boundaries there are many other things you may be concerned about but cannot really influence directly. We exhaust ourselves when we are not clear on the distinction between what we *can* do and what we'd *like* to do.

We have to realize *why* we have a desire to control things. We are the only ones we can control. We must realize we are creatures of projection. We project almost everything we think and feel outside of us. We do it because we are afraid and don't feel safe. We do it to preserve our equilibrium.

Moving from controlling to observing is the simple step that engenders the mindfulness that brings peace to a situation.

Empowerment Exercise: Chimes of Freedom

Tibetan chimes can be found at just about any metaphysical store. They are two bells on a string that make the most lovely sound when they tap against each other. In this exercise, you will let the sound wash over you, calming you. Hold the string at the center, letting each bell hang evenly. Hold it in front of your torso. Let them chime together, and raise your hand slowly up above your head. Feel the chime as the bells rise up your body and across your face. Hear the tone. Let it echo in your ears. Feel the vibration. Receive it. Do this three times.

The Sound of the Bell

Bells have the effect of calming you. A chime says, "It's okay now. All is right." Bells can be used in meditation practice to bring you back to mindfulness. They are a reminder of what is true and what replenishes us. They remind us that we are alive and we are here in this moment, and it is perfect as it is. They get us in touch with the wonder of life and all that is present for us.

You can set up "bells" for yourself throughout the day. These are ways to bring you back to mindfulness. This practice can bring you the calmness and peace that mitigate wear and tear on the body. Think of it as preventative maintenance that keeps you from rushing to the massage therapist for deep tissue massage.

What can work as a "bell" for you? There are many things you can take along with you in your car, your briefcase, at your desk. The sky's the limit. Carolyn has a pyramid of malachite that rests atop her home computer monitor, perfectly centered; at work, she has a pink rock from the Sandia Mountains. Another idea is a small desk fountain with water rippling over slate. The sound of falling water can be very calming. Or in your pocket, you may carry a pebble or something sentimental—something that you touch secretly during the day. Or if you may find that scent anchors you, you may burn candles. Home fragrance kits are available that burn essential oils such as cranberry or lavender.

Then there are the serendipitous "bells" that fall into your day. Carolyn often hears the bells from the Lutheran church playing a hymn just as she leaves the health club across the way. For you, it may be the bells of a church or just the wind in the trees. Finding it is just a matter of tuning in, saying that you will be open to it.

Attachment vs. Nonattachment

We'll let you in on a little secret: Whatever you are most attached to is what you are in most danger of losing. That's because, in the grand cosmic scheme of the Universe, your God is always seeking to get you to turn to Him—not that thing you think you need. Whether it's money, a relationship, a job, or a possession—even if it's good and worthy and brings you joy—it is not real. It is not the true source of joy and peace.

When we gain an understanding of mindfulness and develop a practice, we can begin to recognize that those things or people or beliefs we are so attached to are impermanent. What *is* permanent is your understanding of the Divine—that which transcends the human senses.

The practice of moving from attachment to nonattachment can deepen over a lifetime. Use this journaling exercise to cultivate a technique that you can employ throughout the day any time you hit an attachment issue.

Begin by identifying two or three things that you believe are vital to your future happiness. Examples might be your work, your money, your relationships, or your health: "I want to make more money doing new, creative work." Or "I would like to meet someone I can share my life with." Or "I would like to get my children into a certain school." Whatever it is.

Now write a sentence or two about what is holding you back. Go ahead and just free write. Let 'er rip. If you think it's your boss who is blocking your chance at promotion, put that down.

Once you have made your list, share them with your partner. Hear her list.

Over the next week, as you go about your life, when those thoughts come to you that you must have this or you must have that, bring yourself back to mindfulness, using one of the "bells" you have set up in your day to remind you. Say, "This is not permanent. Divine love is what lasts. Divine love is what I seek." During your next massage session, say out loud each of the items on your list and feel it disengage—detach—from your body, release it, and allow it to float away and dissipate. Allow the peaceful flow of Divine energy to enter your body in its place ... *feel it.*

> Every day we do things, we are things that have to do with peace. If we are aware of our life ..., our way of looking at things, we will know how to make peace right in the moment, we are alive.
> —Thich Nhat Hanh, *Vietnamese Buddhist teacher and author*

Touchstone: Creating Mindfulness

Buddhist teacher Thich Nhat Hanh urges practitioners of mindfulness to carry a pebble in their pockets. Each time the thoughts come that cause suffering, reach into your pocket. Cup it into the palm of your hand. Smooth your fingers across it. He offers three steps for transforming your thoughts. Say, "I am angry. I suffer." Then: "I am doing my best." Then: "Please help me." The pebble is a source of comfort. It grounds you. It reminds you there is a way to do this. It reminds you of the path. It brings you back into the role of observer of your thoughts. The reminder comes through touch.

Mala beads are a tool used by Tibetans in meditation practice. Their purpose is to recite a mantra or affirmation. Some describe them as a portable "sacred space," because you can carry them in your pocket. Just touching them can help you center.

Malas are usually 108 beads and are often made from tulsi (basil) wood, sandalwood, rudraksh seeds, or crystal. Each material is believed to have properties that influence the direction of your meditations. There is always one summit bead called "sumeru." They can be found in metaphysical stores or on the Internet.

To use mala beads, hold them in your right hand in one of two ways. One is between the thumb and ring finger, using the middle finger to rotate each bead toward you with each recitation of your mantra. In the other method, you drape the mala over your middle finger and use your thumb to rotate each bead. Either way, the forefinger is never used to move the bead. Also, the summit bead is never passed over. So if your meditation brings you around to the summit bead, you reverse the rotation.

Other traditions also use beads: Christians (particularly Catholic, Anglican, and Orthodox) use 33 beads, while Muslims use 99 beads, reciting all the names of God.

Low Self-Esteem vs. Healthy Self-Esteem

Being mindful in this area can be the key to experiencing the true joy that life has to offer. When we fill our minds with thoughts about not being good enough, when we focus on past mistakes rather than what we might have learned from a situation, we are only bringing down our esteem for ourselves. The key to this is not to inflate ourselves. That pattern of overinflation and deflation is about as effective as yo-yo dieting. The parallel is bingeing and deprivation. So don't binge out on positive statements about yourself. Nor should you wallow in self-deprecating or limiting thoughts. It's no good to have a case of the "can'ts." Instead, substitute the "not yets." Or choose instead to do what you can do well and do it better. The happy middle ground is acceptance: Sometimes we're good; sometimes we're learning. The constant—the thing you can rely on—is loving yourself as you are in the present moment.

Empowerment Exercise: A Prayer Feather

A prayer feather is a string of beads numbering the years of your life, with a feather at the end. Making a prayer feather is easy. All you need is beading string, enough beautiful and exotic beads to number your years on the planet, and a feather. You may find these at a craft store, or you may want beads from stones of the earth such as quartz, sodalite, hematite, and so on. Gem and mineral stores usually carry these stone beads, along with other symbols that you may find to be meaningful emblems for your life—yin/yang enameled discs or Celtic emblems. Tie your feather to one end, add an emblem if you desire, and start stringing the beads.

Use it much in the way you would mala beads or a rosary for meditation, only each bead represents a year of being you. The feather and any emblem you add should make an overarching statement to you about who you are. The purpose of this meditation is to focus on loving yourself for who you are. As you choose each bead, really *see* your choice. Pay attention to the colors, shapes, and materials. You are combining sight and touch in your experience of the prayer beads. Many gems, stones, and feathers have esoteric meanings and you may want to research this, but remember that your sensory perception is what is most important here—choose based on what *looks, feels, sounds, tastes, and smells* right to you. Take the time to touch your feather, brushing it with your fingertips. Note the patterns in it. The feather represents the complete you. Remember, peacocks eat thorns to make their beautiful plumage. As you touch your feather, think of how all those thorns created a beautiful you. Bring your prayer feather beads to massage sessions with you and feel their quiet power as you give your senses over to the experience of massage.

Map of the Heart

Our senses sometimes lead us to explore the balance of envy versus a belief in plenty. When we let ourselves believe that something someone else has is better than what we have, we have committed a deep injury to ourselves. It's simply not true. Envy is based, first of all, on the perception that someone else is deriving happiness from a *thing*. That may not be true at all. Second of all, it is based on the belief that a *thing* will also make us happy. That also may not be true. Envy, too, often comes from a belief in scarcity—the idea that only a certain few can be allowed to have this *thing* we hold in such esteem. Mindfulness comes first from realizing what we are doing, then gathering new evidence to replace those thoughts. Switch over to a belief in plenty. Write some lines in your Empowerment Journal of replacement thoughts. "I have enough love" or "I have enough money" are examples. Tell yourself: "*I experience joy here, now, simply through touch, taste, smell, hearing, and sight. I breathe. I live.*"

Resentment vs. Grace

Resentment is attachment grown old. Resentment is a negative attitude about a past event. It means you didn't like it when it happened, and you didn't speak your mind. More than likely you held your tongue to keep the peace. But look what happened to your *anger* about what happened: *You kept it.* Resentments can be very unconscious. We may not even realize that we are still hanging on to some event from the past. It may just hook into us without warning and drag us back to what was said, or not said, before. But resentments can really weigh us down, moving into our bodies and refusing to move out as long as we hold onto them.

Bringing mindfulness to resentment means discerning whether it is something small or something big. How big of an obstacle is this for you? How frequently do you encounter it? If it's small, it is time for grace to be brought to the situation. If it's big, ask yourself what is out of balance here—in your life and in how you may have stored your resentments in your body. Ask yourself who is responsible for what. Then ask yourself what you are not bringing to the situation. If it's something where you need to speak what is in your heart, do so. But once done, you will need to let it go. You may or may not be able to change it. The only thing you can do is change your perception and be mindful of your response. During massage sessions, meditate upon the release of resentments. Pay attention to where your body registers pain and release during the session as you do this.

Judging vs. Accepting

When we judge someone, it is often because we cannot accept him or her as is. We are trying to change that person. Many times it's because we're afraid that same quality might exist in some form within us. Instead of focusing on that quality within us, we focus on eradicating that quality in the other person. The first step to accepting someone else is joining with that person. We must see how we are all alike in the most elemental ways. Carolyn has a friend who says, "Remember, we are each of us doing the best that we can at the time." It's a very compassionate stance. It puts us in the place of the other. Have you ever flown off the handle at a comment someone else thought was innocuous? Have you ever stung someone with your words when they didn't deserve it—when the real target was your spouse or your boss who had said something critical the morning before? Have you ever failed to send a thank-you note? Failed to listen better? We have all been there.

Massage is the ultimate release of judging thoughts and sensory perceptions. During massage, *acceptance* is the key to the release of harsh critics, both from within and without. As you allow your body to shed blocks created by internal and external judging comments and/or situations, you may find yourself becoming more open and compassionate in your daily life, and encouraging the same response and respect from others around you.

Now join your hands, and with your hands your hearts.
—William Shakespeare, *King Henry VI*

Empowerment Exercise: Joining

When we join with others, we perceive through our earthly human senses more how we are alike than how we are different. We feel a part of something bigger than ourselves. You can do the following exercise with a partner or a group of friends. Perhaps you have a group with whom you regularly do yoga or meditate. Or perhaps you have a group of friends with whom you feel comfortable discussing spiritual and emotional growth but you have yet to get them together to meditate. Let this book and this chapter spur you to gather that group Sunday morning at daybreak or at the rise of the next full moon. Or let it spur you to take part in a yoga or meditation class.

In yoga or meditation, chanting "om" releases tension and promotes peace. The tension is around the idea that we are separate from each other, that we are too different to bridge the gap, that we are too stubborn and set in our ways, stuck in our "boxes," to form communion with others. The simple chanting of "om" dispels that negative energy. In one magical instant, we see how wrong we were to think so. That joining releases a powerful spiritual vibration. It fills your body with a luminous energy. It says, "Here we are, God, we're all together now." It says, "I am part of the symphony of life. I am at one with my Creator and all He created."

Om contains four separate parts: ah, oh, mmm, and silence. It has several meanings: the Sound of All Sounds, the Sound of the Universe, the Sound of Creation, and the Beginning of Life. It is a pure sound. When you chant "om," your body becomes a resonating chamber.

Sit comfortably with your group with your back straight, shoulders relaxed. Inhale. On the exhalation, chant "om," letting it take hold and build. Let it vibrate in your throat. Remember the four separate parts. Pause. Inhale and exhale. Chant twice more.

And forget not that the earth delights to feel your bare feet and the winds long to play with your hair.

—Kahlil Gibran, from *The Prophet*

Feeling Alive

Some smells can transport us to memories long forgotten. Some tastes are worth more than a stack of frequent flyer tickets. They can take us to Paris or Tahiti or Manhattan. Some clients who come to Erica can cry spontaneously when they experience certain smells. Our memories and emotions are attached to these smells. It's not always something romantic, like woodsmoke on a wintry day evoking an idyllic childhood. For Carolyn, it's Dippity-Do, a gloppy, bubbly pink hair gel available in the 1960s; Vidal Sassoon's Alberto V05; or Breck girls brushing their hair with a 100 strokes to care for their shiny mane of curls. It reminds her of growing up with her four sisters, on Saturday nights when her mother would let her curl her hair for church. Smelly socks make her think of her father sitting in his crimson reclining chair watching Lawrence Welk.

It's often what reminds you of home that brings up those tears: security, nurturing, safety. For some it's clean sheets, bread baking in the oven, or soup simmering on the stove.

Erica often will use essential oils during massage because they have a powerful way of shifting a client's frame of reference. The scents can open up a client's mind to a new level of awareness. Certain oils are known for their relaxing qualities (chamomile), while others are used for their invigorating qualities (peppermint). Ylang ylang is said to abate anger born of frustration, while clary sage mixed in with your massage oil is said to produce euphoria. Essential oils may be blended in your massage oil and rubbed into the skin, or they may be used as scents in conjunction with massage to stimulate the mind and the senses. Scents used in massage oil can cool or warm muscles, depending on their properties.

Scents stimulate the chakras to enhance the experience of meditation and massage.

Another way to create a huge shift in perception is through a smudge stick. Sage smudge sticks are often used in Native American ceremonies. They are sometimes used in the home to purify the home of toxins. You can find sage bundles just about anywhere in Albuquerque, but for the rest of the country, the best bet is a metaphysical store or the Internet. One tradition is to light a sage bundle. Blow out the flame, but let the bundle continue to smolder. Go around your house or another area that you want to purify. Maybe you want to erase memories or you want to change the energy of that place.

Ray of Light: Moving Deeper

Jessica had been coming to see Erica every couple weeks for about three months. One evening she announced it was time for her to move deeper into herself. Jessica is a professional—a lawyer who is very outspoken and very together. Though she is highly verbal, she is not comfortable revealing much about herself. At that time, Erica, too, had been directing her focus to bringing the sacred into the realm of work, and she noticed that she suddenly had a wealth of clients who were business women.

With Jessica's permission, Erica decided to do a breath session combined with bodywork. Until that point, all Jessica had allowed was a basic massage. Jessica had always struggled with the left side of her body. Because Erica sensed that Jessica was having a hard time moving out of her head and into her body, Erica decided to light some sage and smudge the area around her. Right away, Jessica began coughing constantly. The sage was lit for only about 20 seconds. Jessica coughed up mucus, all from her left lung, and continued coughing for 45 minutes. It reminded her that she had pneumonia as a child, most severely in her left lung. When her coughing stopped, she reported that the entire left side of her body felt different than her right. She had emptied out a lot of gunk from her lung. She said it felt open. She said it felt wonderful.

Erica used the sage smudge stick with Jessica two more times. Her right lung also let go after a while, but never to the extent that the left one had. But her lungs did even out. Shortly after that, she was able to manifest the relationship she had always wanted.

The Sensation of Fear

It required a lot of hard work for Jessica to continue to go into the coughing that she knew would happen if Erica burned the sage in her presence. Jessica was willing because her desire to feel more at peace with herself was greater than her fear. We must not let our body sensations stop us from moving inward, past the fear. It's hard, because the body sensations feel so real, more real than our thoughts and ideas. Your body may send the message that your head will break open because it is pounding so hard. Or that you are going to throw up.

But we can push the boundaries. Fear will stop us in any way it can. You know what? If you throw up, you throw up. It's okay. Get over it and move on. Remember Andrew from Chapter 5, who had to stop the massage when he felt nauseated and would not let Erica go deeper? The way to move ahead, to dismantle the fear, is to go through it. It may take being sick. What is really the worst that can happen? Using massage to move through these fears is a dance, playing the line between being gentle with ourselves and being unwilling to allow the fear to stop us.

Ray of Light: The Power of Taste

The sense of taste can be just as powerful as that of smell. Taste works sometimes from the inside out. Your tongue can reflect the chemical balance of your body. During detoxification from alcohol or drugs, some people will have sharp metallic taste come up and out of them.

Beth came to Erica on the fourth day after she had quit smoking. Erica did a lot of breath work with Beth in this session. At a certain point, smoke was coming out of Beth's pores. After a while, the whole room stunk of cigarette smoke. Beth could taste it. Erica could taste it. The sheets smelled like smoke. It was nearly nauseating. Erica continued doing a series of intensive breathing sessions with Beth over the next six weeks until the cigarette smell was released from her body.

New Vision

Using color and visual elements in massage can lead to creating a new purpose. Color is powerful. It has powerful messages in our culture. On an energy level, it is light. Wearing certain colors can accentuate certain frequencies. It can draw certain energies into our bodies. Notice how you feel when you wear pink as opposed to red. (Okay, maybe if you are a guy you don't want to try that experiment.) Notice the difference between wearing subdued, earthy colors like olive or beige and wearing brights such as French blue, violet, or red. (Ties count.)

Color can open up our vision and expand our awareness of what is possible to see. Erica has a client who says she feels like she is on target when she can see in her mind's eye purples or greens. Erica's client Evelyn knows she is on target when she sees colors during massage; she reports that's when she knows she and Erica are on to something good. The colors indicate what level of energy is being worked at any given time.

Empowerment Exercise: Vision Keeper

In this exercise, you and your partner will become vision keepers for each other. As we have moved through these chapters, you probably already have sensed a change within yourself. You are not the same person who started this journey. You may not have all the answers yet, but no doubt the answers to the questions have changed. In creating a vision with your partner, test yourself with these questions:

- Is your career meaningful? If not, is that acceptable to you?
- Are your relationships functioning well? Is there a balance of giving and receiving? If not, are you ready to change that?
- Do you see yourself as a spectator of your life or an active participant?
- Do you have the feeling there is something missing in your life? Is there more than this?
- What is your spiritual and emotional legacy?

We don't expect you to have all the action steps right now. But to these questions, you may now respond with a big "No!" to whether your work is meaningful, and an even bigger "No!" to whether that's okay.

As you know, we can talk all day about what we don't want. But ask your partner what she really, really, really wants to be doing with her life, and feel all the tension drop. She may sigh. She may relax. Or the opposite may happen as we get closer to our dreams—excitement. We should not confuse fear with excitement. Excitement, too, feels a little out of control. Oftentimes when we really look at fear, if we are honest, part of what we are feeling is excitement. Some people react with body tremors. If we notice it's fear and excitement, we can focus on the excitement part, and that can move us through the fear. Take a few moments to exchange answers and record them in your Empowerment Journal. This is your vision. Together, you will be vision keepers for each other.

Live your questions now, and perhaps without knowing it, you will live along some distant day into your answers.

—Rainer Maria Rilke, Austrian German poet

The Sense of Things

By opening up to our senses, and using them in massage, we open doors. The sense of play we can have when we just experience the simple joy of hearing, seeing, tasting, touching, or smelling opens up our curiosity. It expands our awareness. We start asking questions that we may not have asked before. And that is what opens the next door. It takes us exactly where we need to go.

Chapter 9

Meditate, Move, Manifest

Massage is a dance—a sublime interaction between moving and waiting, advancing and retreating, emptying and restoring. At its simplest level, then, massage is a dance of energy. Massage is what *moves* the energy. So far, we have drawn upon meditation in many of the massage exercises for this book.

In this chapter, we will show you how stillness and movement work in concert. When you tune into the interplay of stillness and movement, you can boost the healing power of massage. You can manifest what you seek. You can become more congruent, more vibrant, more joyful.

Welcome to the Dance

When we talk about movement being used with massage, we mean two things. One, you can use movement in conjunction with massage therapy—through yoga practice, tai ch'i, or dance, for example. A massage therapist also can be the "dancer," as with lomi lomi massage or Reiki. In this case, the massage therapist is doing a dance with the energy in the room, moving it through your body. But the essence of massage itself, the manipulation of muscles and tissues, is the true energy dance.

Erica often draws upon her background in dance during massage. She started out in ballet at four years old and danced all the way up through college. At some point, she shifted from classic ballet to modern dance because she enjoyed modern dance's openness to interpretation and more organic movement. Classic ballet is a form you fit your body into; modern dance is expression from within. Erica is very aware of where fear resides in the body; out of that experience, she has a deep appreciation for the joy of movement—and the healing work it can do when used with massage.

Let your life lightly dance on the edges of Time like dew on the tip of a leaf.
—Rabindranath Tagore, Indian poet

Ray of Light: For a Dancer

One of Erica's newest clients is Janice, a professional dancer for 20 years. Janice came to Erica just as she was shifting away from classical ballet to explore new forms of movement. Erica found that Janice was able to accelerate her healing because of her natural understanding of movement. Because both share a joy of movement and feel at home with energy moving within their bodies, massage therapist and client truly connect. Erica can be massaging Janice's feet and feel a band of energy through her feet, up her ankle, to her knee, up through her pelvis to her heart, and Janice is already aware of it, too.

Though Janice is charting new territory as she does body work with Erica, she is familiar with the process of movement and trusts it. As a result, Janice experiences incredibly deep openings. The energy moves quickly through her body because it doesn't meet resistance for long. Janice is acquainted with where fear resides in her body, and she already has many years of training herself to work through pain. She knows immediately what Erica means when she advises Janice to drop into the pain. For Janice, the process is condensed: When she encounters old energy patterns, she quickly relaxes, breathes into the pain, then releases.

Erica felt a split in Janice's body. In classic ballet, the emphasis is on extension, to create long lines with a lot of upward movement, but also on opening, hyperextending arms and legs. Janice's presence in her body was in her arms and legs and from her chest up. Her core—her solar plexus or power center—just didn't register. Janice's body energy was flighty and airy. Erica set about to make these two energies meet—reconnecting Janice's upper body to her legs.

Each time Erica saw Janice, Janice became more powerful, more in harmony, congruent, acting with more authenticity and integrity. She became more grounded. Emotional issues in her life started being resolved very quickly.

What Is Movement?

It doesn't matter which form of movement we use. It can be massage, dance, exercise, sex, or a heart-to-heart talk. Acupressure, acupuncture, or herbs can produce energy movement. All of this is movement.

Why does movement work? Pure and simple, it's about joy. Think of an "a-ha" moment you have experienced, and remember the joy you felt. Think of how magnificent that idea was. Think how grateful you were to receive it. Movement is about getting unstuck. You are freed of pain. You leave the darkness behind. It's about clarity. You have a new vision. It's like getting a new windshield for your car. It's like tearing off a new page on your calendar. It's like walking into a new house with big open windows and skylights. You let the light flow in.

Children love to spin until they are dizzy. Think of a child as she dances. She dances like no one is watching. She dances to express how she feels inside. In Sufism, some mystics create the whirling dervish to summon the experience of God. Spinning makes you dizzy and disorients you. When you whirl around, you get your heart rate up, you get the blood pumping through your body, your body temperature rises, you sweat. You are altered. Everything is moving. You become open to expansion. Your eyesight loosens up a bit. You disengage from seeing distinct shapes and identifying them. You begin to see differently. Next time you are stuck on a big life decision, assign yourself some spinning time. See what shifts it creates for you. Notice how it feels in your body. Do you feel looser? Do some of the things you thought mattered no longer matter?

At the same time spinning can make you loosen up, it also defines your center. When you spin, centrifugal force is at work, pulling all the things that don't define the core you to the outside. Those things rotate rapidly around your center, in a blur. Think of a ride at the fair—you know, the one with the spinning teacups. You are pushed to the outside, spinning around the core. If you try to resist being pushed to the edge of the teacup, you feel something push you back. You can *feel* the center. Think of the line of an ice skater as she spins. Visually, you see her elongate, as though a string is being pulled up through her. As her hands dance above her head, her arms seem to meld into one. The center is becoming stronger.

Empowerment Exercise: Spin, Spin, Spin

Try starting off a massage session with spinning, and see what happens. Just spin, spin, spin. Then climb onto the massage table. Start face up, and let your massage partner work on your belly and chest, moving up into your shoulders, neck, and head. Notice the difference in your body. It may feel as though you have started a little farther into a massage session, because you may be more relaxed.

Ray of Light: Spinning Your Wheels

If you'll remember in Chapter 7, we discussed Scott, who is in constant movement. Erica sees that all this movement is his protection, keeping him in his head and keeping him as an observer to his pain, avoiding being it and feeling it. It's Scott's style to tell Erica about the pain rather than feel it. He may moan during a painful point during massage, but even this keeps the pain in the mental arena. She senses that in his case, it's a thought, "I am vocalizing the pain now." And the thought immediately crowds out the feeling.

This is not to say that all clients who vocalize their way through painful points are doing what Scott is doing. Vocalizing can be an excellent way to move through the pain. Erica's intuition guides her in pinpointing the subtle difference between Scott's approach and that of someone like Janice, who so easily drops into the pain. It's the difference between thinking about it, identifying it, labeling it, categorizing it, analyzing it—and just feeling it.

Body Over Matter

Scott has too much mind over matter. Of course, most of the time in our culture we think this is a good thing. Our conditioning is to activate our minds to block out pain. We bite the bullet. We endure. We tell ourselves the pain isn't real. We tell ourselves it isn't really happening. We use our minds to club the pain over the head. Hmmm ... think about this. This is fighting pain with more pain. Pain is the enemy. This kind of mind over matter, without transcendence, leads to repressed emotions, deep-seated anger, or just plain numbness.

Erica has a client who has no kinetic sense of self. He is so in his mind that he tries to think his way through every physical exertion. He is not graceful or artful in his movements. He came to Erica saying he needed to learn how to relax. Often, his entire neck and head would freeze up and he could not move. His talent for focusing on mind over matter often operates at the expense of suppressing his feelings, shutting himself off from the experience of authentic joy. Years of mind training brought him to the point where he could walk on a broken bone and not feel the pain, but his body is yearning for a shift, to open up to a new way of coping.

In the case of a woman in labor—and in the case of so many of us when we fight pain—what needs to happen is *body over matter*. The body knows what to do. The pain serves a purpose. Labor and childbirth coaches tell women to envision each contraction doing the most work it can do. They coach women to embrace the pain—because it has work to do. More pain, more progress.

Know that the body understands how to heal its pain. It knows how to release the tightness in the muscles. It knows how to open up the places with stored-up pain. Each time you have a massage, your body is waiting for that moment when the touch of the massage therapist will activate the pain and release it. Each time the massage therapist touches you, the body takes in the energy and sends it exactly where it needs to go. That is precisely why it is so scary. But trust it. Move with it; open up and release into it.

When a woman is in the throes of labor, her mind is saying, "I can't do this. What am I going to do? How am I going to get out of this?" Her mind is panicked. It feels trapped. There is a lot of anguish. When Erica was in labor with one of her three sons, the midwife told her, "Let

157

your body do it. The body knows how. It's just that the mind is frightened." At that point (the midwife reminded her a few times), Erica would drop into her body. She would let out a horrific, gut-wrenching moan. Then there would be release around the contraction, and Erica would move into it. When she surrendered her mind, her body knew what to do. When we stop resisting pain, we can allow ourselves to feel the movement of the energy. It may well hurt, but it doesn't matter. It's moving. Let it happen.

Empowerment Exercise: Fire and Ice

For this two-part exercise, we will first borrow on an exercise from childbirth preparation classes that Carolyn took with midwife and author Pam England (*Birthing from Within*), who teaches that birth is a spiritual experience, not a medical event. The class was oriented to training expectant moms to face the pain and sink into it, avoiding the drugs that often intensify the pain and slow down the labor. Use this exercise before a massage session—perhaps one that you are coming into with a lot of chronic pain—and experience the difference that body-over-matter training can have on a massage.

Get a large basin and fill it with cold water, adding ice cubes. Beforehand, summon an image in your mind, a pleasant image, something that brings you comfort. Plunge your hand into a bowl of icy water. Keep your hand in the icy water for 30 seconds. It's a long time, believe us, for the first 30 seconds! The icy water can be a shock, even if you already know the water will be cold. Call up your image. Remember to breathe. Focus on your breath. Allow your mind to receive the acknowledgment of the pain. Don't shut it out. Hear your mind scream to remove your hand. Feel the tingling sensation in your bones, your blood. Feel the icy sting of the water. Keep breathing. After 30 seconds, remove your hand.

Build up to one minute, two minutes, then three. Notice how you are able to tolerate more pain as you increase the time. Notice as you are breathing through it how you feel about the pain. Notice that you no longer think of the pain as something to fight. Notice how you accept it. Notice how you let it stay. Notice how it starts to change. It lessens. Notice how you start to feel more powerful than the pain. Now pull your hand out of the bowl.

For the second part of this exercise, we will do a Belly Fire Breath massage. Start by lying on your back, with your massage partner on your right side, by your liver. The liver is a Fire organ in traditional Chinese medicine, and the seat of anger. Caution: If you have any kind of liver disease, do not do this exercise.

The massaging partner places his left hand on your heart, to ease and balance the Fire coming up. He rests the palm of his hand at the bottom of your rib cage. Breathe through your mouth in intense, fast exhales, punching your breath out, three times. Take a slow deep breath. With each exhale, the massaging partner, pushes into your diaphragm. Do this three times on each side. End it with the massaging partner sliding his hands to grip the sides of the torso, pulling up. Close by having him place one hand on your heart (fourth chakra), the other on your belly (third, or power, chakra).

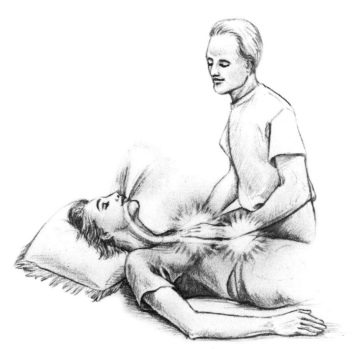

Belly Fire Breath massage brings a lot of clarity to your head and eyes, changing your vision.

The Role of Meditation

Why, you may wonder, do we use meditation exercises in conjunction with massage? You may have already detected the magic inherent in the exercises you have done so far. Meditation brings forth a radiance from within. When you sink into meditation and all the other "monkey-mind" thoughts are shut out, you sink into a glow. It's the pure life-force energy. You remember how alive you truly are.

How do we define meditation? Erica used to be pretty hard on herself because her days of giving massage, appointment after appointment, would prevent her from carving out special time for meditation during the average day. After all, she was setting herself up as a spiritual guide and teacher through massage. But a therapist told her, "Erica, your whole day is a meditation. All day long." The lights went on. "Oh, you're right," Erica said. "That is the space I'm in."

Meditation does not have to occur sitting on a pillow in the lotus position. Meditation is a state of being. Meditation can occur when we are working with our hands. So many of us in this day and age engage in thinking and planning, talking and meeting—strategizing—for most of our work days. Day after day, we hear stories of people who are downsizing their lives, chucking the corporate life for 20 acres and a plow or just cashing in the 401(k) and starting a bakery. In the urban-suburban high-tech world, we yearn for the simple act of doing something with our hands. We yearn to make things. Erica is fortunate that she spends her day working with her hands. This is her meditation.

Map of the Heart

Take a few moments to reflect in your Empowerment Journal about the ways that meditation occurs naturally in your daily life. If you work with your hands, say a blessing or prayer of gratitude for this gift. In practicing meditation, whether in formal ways or throughout your day, you lay the groundwork for meditation to be used during a massage session. The practice will heighten your experience of massage.

Meditating is another way of hooking up with the Source, when we allow the Divine to speak to us. When you meditate, all the other stuff drops away. Your mind may fight it. No doubt if you have sat in the lotus position, or if you have spent time writing in your Empowerment

Journal, you are all too aware of the press of "monkey mind"—the ego—pelting you with all sorts of reasons why you can't discard that thought. But when you keep still, when you just present yourself as a presence in the face of "monkey mind," not fighting it and not succumbing, what happens—in just one or two more thoughts—is that monkey mind drops away. And then you are left with the purity of your thoughts. You are left with the truth. You are left with a live connection to the Source. It is rapturous.

That live connection is like a broadband Internet connection to Wisdom. This is where the information floods in. You know the steps to take to manifest your visions. Manifestation is bringing visions to physical form. Buy the house. Take the job. Take a chance on that man or woman in your life. What is the next step? You know. What do I want and how do I get there? You know. You don't even have to ask anymore.

Stillness and the Space Between

Many spiritual practices rely on creating inner stillness. From that stillness, we are open to receive the power of our Creator and the wisdom of our Master. Stillness, then, creates the reservoir of personal power. From that still space inside you, you may visit, again and again, the inner temple of your God.

While you are receiving a massage, a disturbing noise can be as helpful as silence. When you are meditating and drawing in stillness, a disturbing noise brings up an inner resistance. When you allow it to be as it is, when you neither resist nor ignore the noise, when you simply let it be in your space, the resistance drops. You do not see the noise as an enemy, a force outside of you. In dropping the resistance, you join with it. This acceptance allows you to drop into inner peace.

Attuning your hearing to the higher level of hearing also means paying just as much attention to the gaps between sounds. Remember that there are four parts to chanting "om," the sound of all sounds—ah, oh, mmm, and silence. In any atom there is space between the nucleus and the electrons, space from one electron to the next. When the energy level of an electron suddenly alters, it leaps that space. Think about it: Built into the building blocks of the universe, there is space.

The space in between is the stillness that we all seek, the stillness that is the wellspring for a higher level of attunement. Take time to notice the space between words in a conversation. Listen for the space between the musical notes as you hear a piano or guitar played. Note the stillness between in-breath and out-breath.

> Meditation, then, is bringing the mind home.
> —Sogyal Rinpoche, Buddhist teacher

Empowerment Exercise: The Ripple Effect, Plus Cobra

Before your next massage session with your partner, try this meditation and yoga's Cobra pose that follows it for one week. See what a difference it makes in the way you experience your next session.

Sit comfortably. Breathe in and out three times. Bring your awareness to the present moment. Settle into your breathing and direct your awareness to what is happening in your body. Let your breath glide up and down your spine. Release all thoughts that pull you out of the present. Allow yourself to listen to the sounds within your body. Hear yourself breathe. Sit with that a few moments. Now move your awareness out to the next layer of sound—those within about 10 feet of your body. Listen to each sound. Is the clock ticking? Is the computer humming? After two or three minutes, move out to the next layer of sound—about 25 yards out. Sit, breathe and listen. Is there anyone else in the house with you? Are there children playing nearby? Is the washing machine running? Did a car go by? Listen deeply, focusing on these sounds. Now move your focus out beyond the 25 yards. How far can you hear? At what point does it cease to be sound and become sense-intuition? Pure awareness? How far can you open your awareness and discern life?

We recommend you try this meditation both inside and outside. Have fun. Play with this exercise and invent variations of your own. Notice how you have to deepen into a place of stillness to expand to the outward distances. Notice that the farther out you want to go, the deeper in you must focus.

Yoga's Cobra pose holds within it the dichotomy of stillness and movement. It is a very enlivening pose, with lots of opening. At the same time you are being still, you are stimulating lots of energy movement within the body.

Yoga's Cobra pose.

Lie face down on your yoga mat with your feet together and toes pointed. Place your palms at about chest level and hold your elbows parallel to your torso. Tighten your legs and buttocks. Envision the lower half of your body as the locked cobra tail.

As you inhale, slowly raise your head, chin, neck, shoulders, and chest, gently contracting your back muscles. Keep your shoulders down and relaxed. If you feel them moving up to your ears, let them sink down. Lift your head and chest as high as you comfortably can. Look up, ahead and out to the room. Hold it for three to six breaths. Slowly roll down.

This pose relies on your back muscles for the lift. Don't use your arms to push your body up; merely use them to steady yourself. This pose helps to align and strengthen your spine.

The Sound of Music

Erica often uses music in conjunction with massage because it helps us to connect to the flow and lift out of all those things that slow us down and cloud our vision. Music can give the mind something to focus on so that it has something to do while the body is doing its natural healing work during a massage. Music engages us emotionally. It can soothe us. It can stimulate us visually. It can inspire us, lifting us out of the mundane. Music can create a huge shift. It can jolt us out of the ruts we have been in. It has been said the only difference between a rut and a coffin is that a coffin has ends. That's the role music can play when we hit a crossroads and we stand there, in a quandary about which road to take. It lifts us out of the tiny little boxes we create for ourselves. It helps us remember there is a bigger world beyond ourselves and our daily problems.

Erica has a collection of music that she uses in her massage sessions. She uses primarily instrumental because she finds that words distract, or she will play music that uses the voice as an instrument, as in chants. She finds that certain music will move the emotions, while other music will direct her work to the visceral. Strings and piano bring up emotions, while drums and other percussion emphasize physical work. Often she uses richer music, with soothing strings, long phrasing, and rich melodies to create a safe, nurturing environment. When a client needs to open his vision, she might use the Native American flute. It's very still, a clear, high, open sound with lots of vibration. It helps the mind expand. Still other clients like the sound of the ocean. The sound of waves can bring forth a lot of energy movement.

At a Crossroads

As Erica and Carolyn were writing this chapter, as it would happen, both were feeling stuck about decisions they needed to make in their lives. Carolyn was thinking about buying a house (she did!), and Erica was grappling with a personal decision. Carolyn was debating about whether to move forward into the unknown, while Erica was weighing whether to get an ending begun. Both felt they were in a holding pattern as they waited for the signal to move forward. Erica felt she had been standing at the crossroads for some time, knowing which road to take. For her it was a balance of listening and acting, that same balance between stillness and movement.

Touchstone: Salt Glow Massage

When you are stuck, turn to salt. A salt bath or salt rub can be the key to breaking through it.

Salt is a powerful purifier. It opens us up to the sensual world. Our sense of taste is heightened with a little salt. When you sauté vegetables and add a little salt, they get juicier. Salt releases what is on the inside to the outside. The flavor comes out. Yeah, we know all the research about high blood pressure. But this is on your skin. Let it go. Salt opens you. Open yourself up. Let your flavor come out.

Buy some sea salts from your natural foods store. Carolyn uses vanilla herbal sea salts with gingko and Celtic sea salt from Sunshine Spa. The night before another massage session with your partner, take a hot bath with sea salt and baking soda. Use one cup each of baking soda and sea salt in hot water. Soak for 15 minutes. The salt acts like a poultice, sucking lactic acid out of your body. This has the effect of cleansing and purifying the energy of your body. When you are congested—whether that means having a bad cold or just being stuck emotionally—it will clear things out. This is a great bath to take when you are simply exhausted, feeling overly toxic or emotionally stuck. Make it fun. Light candles. Slide down in the tub so that your neck and shoulders absorb the warmth of the water. Afterward, as the water is draining out of the tub, stand up and shower off. It's important to wash the salt away from your skin.

For the next massage session with your partner, rub the salts all over your partner's body, working in clockwise circular motions. Start with him face down. Using the salts, move up his left leg, starting at the bottom of his foot, spiraling clockwise all the way to his neck and back of his head. Repeat on the right side. Again, remember to shower off, washing the salt off your skin afterward.

Let yourself be open and life will be easier. A spoon of salt in a glass of water makes the water undrinkable. A spoon of salt in a lake is almost unnoticed.
—Buddha

When you are at a crossroads, incorporate techniques of stillness and movement into massage sessions with your partner. Use some of these exercises as a prelude, then bring to your massage session the intention to move the energy. In giving a massage to your partner, focus your awareness on the way energy moves, then rests, in her body. For instance, one technique is to press as your partner exhales, then move. When she exhales completely, stop. Rest during her inhale. When she releases, press again, move up her body.

Manifesting What You Seek

How can you manifest what you want in your life? In this four-part exercise, we will guide you through steps that you can use again and again to bring it forth. You will meditate, move, massage, and manifest.

Step One: Your Heart's Desire

For this meditation, sit in a comfortable position with your eyes closed. Bring the thumbs and forefingers of each hand together to form a triangle. Hold it in front of your heart. Relax your elbows. Inhale through your nose and exhale through your mouth. Do this for a count of eight. As you breathe, envision a current of energy flowing through your heart center. Envision your hands as a channel receiving it and directing it. See it as a continuous current. Say aloud, "What is my heart's desire?"

Wait, breathe, and listen carefully. When you have received a response, hold it there in your mind's focus, breathing the current through your heart. Envision your hands holding a space for that intention to form and flourish in your body.

Map of the Heart

Make a few notes in your Empowerment Journal of what you have manifested in your life—the good, the bad, and the ugly. If you have lots of love in your life but a bad credit rating, put that down. You created that. You get credit for both. If you have career and financial success in spades but haven't found your life and love partner, put that down.

Step Two: The Energy Dance

In the Energy Dance, there are no rules. The only rule is free-form movement. Whatever way you feel like moving is the right way. You may want to do it to music. You may want to dance with scarves. You may want to light candles. You may want to dance with a small drum, maracas, or bells. Or you may want to do all of the above.

Focus on the root chakra first, working up. Breathe and move according to how the energy you are focused on feels in your body. Stomp your feet on the floor. Call up the energy. Say, "Dance with me!"

As you move up to the heart chakra, focus your attention on the energy of love. Focus on your heart, your chest, your back. The secret with each chakra is to be willing to move with the energy. Let go of caring whether you look foolish or artless. Let yourself feel it all, as you focus on each energy moving up through you.

Open up the chakras with the Energy Dance.

With practice, you will find that you enjoy some chakras more than others, that some open up more readily while others don't. With practice, each one will open up sooner. Envision yourself on the surface of the ocean, with great white waves. Notice how they bob against the sky.

Envision yourself swimming in the ocean, alongside the dolphins, arcing out of the water, sunlight glimmering on the droplets of sea. Dive deeper, under the surface, with the sunlight and shadow reflecting off the surface. Follow a school of fish. And then, we have the option of diving even deeper, to swim with the whales, to know the other creatures that only live in the depths of the ocean. This may be why we love whales: They are the keepers of the deep.

Step Three: Massage, the Portal

Massage is the doorway through which you can swim with the big boys. It's only a matter of what depth you will allow yourself. Do a series of manifestation massages with your partner over a two-week period, one right after the other, using toning during the session. With your partner standing at your feet, have him place his hands on your soles. Take a deep breath, just see what sound comes out. Play with the tones. Notice how they vibrate in your body. Play with vowel sounds, then move up and down the scale. See what happens. Notice from one massage to the next the limitations and fears that come up. Determine what you are ready to release now. Envision the whale leading you through the depths of the ocean. Allow yourself to go as deep as you can go.

Step Four: Manifesting

Remember in Chapter 3 when we discussed the five directions in Native American spirituality, their animal spirit, and their elements? Aligned with each is a manifestation, the way that energy is manifested in the world. For the south it is music; for west, magic; for east, art and writing; for north, philosophy, religion and science; for the center, spirituality. Take a few moments to refer to that table. Note the enemies of that energy: fear, powerlessness, death and old age, certainty, and inertia. What is your demon? What is holding you back from manifesting your heart's desire? Pick one and take a few moments in your Empowerment Journal to write about how it blocks your way and your vision. Now choose a word from the list to use as a tool. Maybe you know it is fear that keeps you from moving forward. Maybe you know it is a sense of powerlessness. Now ask yourself how you can tap into your own magic. Give yourself an assignment: to paint, to write, to pray, to play music. Do that with an intensity of focus for two weeks.

Like the winds of the sea are the winds of fate / As we voyage along through life, / Tis the set of the soul that decides its goal / And not the calm or the strife.

—Ella Wheeler Wilcox, American writer and poet

The Big Wide Ocean

With meditation, we open to vastness. We call upon that which is greater than our earthly perspective. The ego-mind is a drop of the ocean as opposed to the whole ocean. Meditating allows us to play in the deep sea. We may feel small as we ride the swell of a wave. But when we allow ourselves to feel the fear and excitement of the vast ocean, we can be a part of a much greater reality.

What is manifestation? A healthier you. A meaningful relationship. A bigger house. A reliable car. A project completed. A contract signed. Children with their own strong wills. A broken home that became a whole home. New ways of thinking. A more accepting society. The creation of your true passion. All this and more are what we create when we manifest our desires.

Energy never goes anywhere. It only changes form. When we move energy through massage or movement, we are not adding, nor are we shedding, energy. What we are doing with massage, meditation, and movement is learning how to form the energy into the shapes we want. Massage again and again relaxes the body and mind so we can bring the energy through faster. Instead of waiting a month or a year or a decade, you can see massage manifest the energy creations right before your eyes.

Part Four

Hands-On Healing

In this next series of chapters, we move through massage into the deepest healing of all. As you approach the center, your Divine essence, you will begin to see more openings ahead, more light. Your work here represents the movement toward the attainment of enlightenment. This is the way we are allowed the approach to the hallowed inner circle. Here at the center, with a heart that is opening, lifting, becoming lighter, you are in an open state of devotion. Ahead, we will show you how massage creates these openings, how acceptance of ourselves and intimacy with another create an expanded vision that reaches beyond the mundane, physical world, beyond the mind and the emotions, to the plane of the spiritual—and the eternal.

Chapter 10

Opening to Acceptance

Massage is a dance of acceptance. The therapist must accept the receiver as she is. The receiver must accept the therapist. For the therapist, it means relinquishing judgments and letting go of being attached to an outcome for the receiver. For the receiver, it takes an incredible amount of surrender. This is why there is such magic in the merging. Without that, it's just two hands rubbing a body. It has no depth, no healing capabilities, no infinite within it.

In this chapter, we will introduce you to polarity therapy as a path to opening up to acceptance of self and other. We will guide you in using massage to remove blocks and get to the true source of your fear. We will help you achieve alignment, closing the gap between your perceived self and your true self, integrating all parts of you. Emerging from this acceptance, you will find you have a strong, intact core.

All of Me

Acceptance of self is the key to inner peace, but it's so much easier said than done.

A few years ago, Carolyn wanted to lose some weight—about 12 pounds—because she thought she would look and feel better. This time, she decided that she wasn't willing to wait until she shed the pounds to feel good and accept herself. She was tired of the thoughts running through her mind each morning when she put on her clothes and they didn't fit—you know, thoughts like "Oh what a blob I am" and "I have no will-power. Why did I eat that?"

She decided to short-circuit those thoughts. Instead, she decided she would have the acceptance thoughts *now*, before she shed the pounds. So every time she looked in the mirror, she would say "I am working on losing 12 pounds, and I know I will like the way I look then. But I like myself now. I like this body, too." This acceptance was a big shift for her. Dieting no longer felt punitive.

This time it no longer came from that place of disliking the way she was at the moment. It came from the place of loving all of herself, flabby and thin. As a result, the 12 pounds she lost were effortless. She isn't even quite sure when she hit her goal. She just knows that at a certain point, her clothes felt better and people were complimenting her.

The Art of Grateful Acceptance

Acceptance can bridge the gap between enemies—in this case, Carolyn and her heavier body. Or it could be pain and your body, sadness and your mind, the person who hurt you and yourself. When you see the person who hurt you as being like yourself, you have compassion for her. You stop fighting her. And when you stop fighting her, she no longer has the power to hurt you.

Acceptance is about making peace with the dichotomy, seeing the two opposites as part of a whole. Stillness flows into movement and back into stillness. Joy flows into sadness and back to joy. It's the yin flowing into the yang. It's the natural process of life.

Empowerment Exercise: Making Peace with Imperfection

This massage exercise draws upon polarity therapy, which works with negative and positive energy flows. We all have energy moving through our bodies through strands of energy—like highways. Each energy has a positive pole and negative pole like a battery. Energy patterns get disrupted through trauma, pain, or fear.

The therapist uses his or her own body to connect positive and negative points on the other person's body to re-establish the flow. In polarity therapy, left and right are important, so heed that in the following directions.

Before starting, set your intention. Sitting across from your partner, share what you want to accept about yourself. Say aloud, "I want more understanding about ..." State your intention to expand your experience to understand both sides of this dichotomy within you. Your goal is to use this massage to broaden your perspective so that you can comfortably hold this duality about yourself. In the example of loving and hating your body, for instance, you might say you love the strength of your body and its power to move. You might say you hate that it's bigger than what's deemed "acceptable" in our culture. You might say you have always felt not good enough because of your body. It's important to bring forward all parts of the duality. Be as specific as possible. It is also vital to say it out loud. Feel all the ripples reverberate through you as you speak of what you love and what you hate.

The receiving partner starts on his tummy. The giving partner stands on the right side of the table, facing the right side of the receiving partner's body. Put your right hand on his left shoulder blade and your left hand on his right buttocks. This connects the head energy in the neck and shoulders with the source energy in the gluteal muscles and pelvis. So you are working with the negative end of the pole in the buttocks and the positive end of the pole in the top of the spine. Start off slow, with a deep long rocking movement, building toward a crescendo, using faster, more aggressive movement. When you hit the crescendo, let it subside and sink into stillness. Experiment with it. What does it feel like when you hit a groove? At what point does it feel like you moved into your partner's deep rhythm, finding the place where he vibrates? You'll know because it will feel comfortable to you in your hands. Once you hit that place where it is smooth and right, do it for 30 seconds, then stop.

With your right hand, find all those trigger points between the shoulder blade and the spine. Move into stimulating movements—the pitta, or fire, from the ayurvedic tradition. Use quick, short pushes into all these points. You are stirring up the energy. Your movements get hotter, faster. During this, keep your left hand resting on his hip.

Then using your left hand, mirror the "pitta" motions on the buttocks. Move your fingers around the edge of the sacrum. As you slide your hand down the sacrum, feel the edge of it. Move your fingers deep into the gluteal muscles. As he exhales, press. During this part, keep your right hand on his shoulder blade.

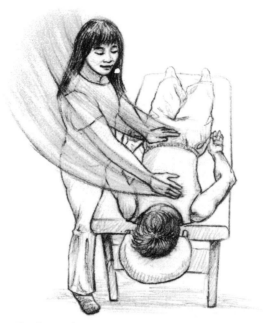

Rocking polarity.

Move back and forth between the shoulder blade and hip a few times. As you are stimulating the shoulder blade, notice when you feel heat in the opposite hand. This confirms the connection has been made.

Return to the rocking motion at the hip. Start off gentle, then faster. Slow to a gentle rock. Feel the flow between the hip and shoulder. Use the information coming through your hands as a barometer. When you feel a tingle, or a steady heat, then you know you have a clear connection.

Repeat from the left side. With polarity therapy it is always important to do each exercise from both sides.

To end the session, move down and put palms of your hands on the soles of his feet. The receiving partner should say, "I am as I am." This is a very powerful heart-to-heart connection. It's very unifying because there is equal pressure on the positive and negative. Stay in this position until you feel a steady heat flow.

It's Unacceptable

We can know for decades that we need to accept a situation as it is, and we can even think we have, only to find out we're still trying to change it. We can walk around for years trying to change other people's minds and there is still one person who hurt us in our childhood who is the person we are really trying to change. Some of that is about channeling hurt in a positive way. A man whose brother's life is in ruins because of alcoholism becomes a great spiritual teacher. A woman who was sexually abused becomes a lawyer taking on class-action suits on behalf of other women. A man whose childhood was riddled with secrets becomes a journalist crusading for the truth, exposing corruption.

Think about who you are still trying to change. You may be actively trying to change that person. It may be a parent, or a child.

What Can't You Accept?

When you examine the source of your greatest pain, what is behind that? Was there not enough love? Could you never gain the approval of a parent? Was a sibling favored over you? Did something bad happen, an external event such as war or divorce or bankruptcy that altered the course of your life and seemed to limit your choices?

Shift your attention to some of the positive effects of that event in your life. Maybe a divorce meant that you moved to live near an aunt you dearly loved. Maybe it forged a strong bond with a sibling. Maybe you responded to abuse by turning to art or writing, creating a rich inner life. Maybe it meant you married later because you were more cautious about relationships and when you found someone, it was a more rewarding, lasting relationship. Maybe poverty made you a crusader or a hard worker. How were you served by these difficult, forging events?

Map of the Heart

Write in your Empowerment Journal about what resulted because of your life-course changing event. Write everything, both good and bad. Now write a line describing the event as a statement in your Empowerment Journal. "Mom didn't love me, and I can't change that." Or "My parents split up, and I can't change that." Or "When I was six, my family left my country of birth to start over in the United States. And I can't change that." Or "When my mother died, my father never got over the loss and we kids knew it. And I can't change that."

Share what you wrote with your massage partner. Together, repeat these affirmations: "I choose to release the past that holds me stuck in all that was. I choose to move with love into the unknown. I choose to rest in the faith of myself as master."

Empowerment Exercise: Removing the Blocks

This massage can be done with you lying on your back or tummy. Begin by saying, "I am willing to move through any blocks that are appropriate to release today."

As your massaging partner works different areas of your body, breathe and relax into it. After a few minutes, ask the giving partner what she senses in your body. Listen openly to what she says. Ask out loud, "Where am I holding on? What am I holding onto?" Speak the answers out loud. Consider the feedback your massaging partner has given and how you feel about it. Let yourself fall back into the massage, breathing and relaxing as your partner continues. Open yourself to discern what the next level of letting go is about. Do a check-in two or three times more during the massage. Be as honest as you can about what had you feeling uncomfortable.

Ray of Light: Getting to the Source of Fear

In previous chapters, we have mentioned clients who come to Erica for healing but won't let themselves go completely into the pain. They have blocks that feel too scary. Some of them are conscious of the blocks and are aware of how they are limiting their healing. Others just can't push past it. Others truly lack any experience of surrender in their past that worked. They have no reference point for letting go. The fear grips them too tightly. They see it as just too real. The key to getting to the source is first having the experience of the sweetness of surrender. Some of the exercises we developed in Chapter 7 lay the foundation for establishing a successful experience with surrender. You may find it useful to return to them as we move through these questions.

Answer these questions with your partner in a discussion session prior to massage:

- Where in your body is the source of your greatest pain? Is it in your heart? Your thighs? Your solar plexus?

- If you had to name this pain's emotion, what would it be? Fear? Hurt? Sorrow?

- If you had to hook a memory with this emotion, what would it be? Think of who said it or did it. Think how old you were and what you looked like, what clothes you wore and how your hair was cut. Think what year it was and where you were living.

- If you had to sum up what you learned from the experience, what would it be? What part of this no longer serves you?

When the Pain Is Fresh

If your discovery is new, the pain may be too fresh for you to see any good out of it. You may think, "I can never accept this." You may be grieving so much that you can't see the way out of it. Or there may be so many layers that it's just too scary. You may be afraid there is so much more.

Slow down, take a deep breath and trust in the process. Go one step at a time. The massage exercises in this book are meant to be a guide to open you to the role of massage in healing. If the emotional pain is raw right now, you may want to work with a psychotherapist in conjunction with a massage therapist, as many of the clients who come to Erica do.

When you are truly hurting, you need to take time just to hurt. Let yourself be sad. Let yourself cry. Think you are done with it, and cry some more. Don't go it alone. Know there is somewhere to store the tears, *and it's not in your body.* Make a vow not to keep your hurt within you. Release it with no concern about whether the grief grows. Allow life to reabsorb it. Change and transform your grief into living, vibrant, life-affirming energy.

The idea came to me that I *was, am* and *will be*, but perhaps will not *become*. This did not scare me. There was for me in *being* an intensity I did not feel in *becoming*.

—Nine Berberova, Russian-born poet

Lining It Up

Alignment means bridging the gap between who you are and who you want to be or who you were. It means that all the parts of you—the person you were, the person you are now, and the person you are becoming—are one. Acceptance is the key to embracing all of those parts of yourself—and in truth, the path to becoming is not going forward but going backward, integrating all those parts of yourself you don't want to accept. When you are in alignment with that, you are in your power. You have courage. You are authentic.

In the shamanic tradition, the shaman was the member of the tribe who possessed the power to receive information and transform himself. He could transport himself into other realms. The shaman was a wise person who was a conduit of information for the tribe, telling the others about other shapes, other dimensions. We imagine his job was to get tribeswomen and tribesmen out of the box. The shaman has the ability to change shape. As we move through the exercises ahead, we will invoke the energy of the shaman: We will align with other energies and take a new form.

Often clients in massage sessions will tell Erica they took the form of an animal spirit. Dolphins probably come up the most frequently. They are seen as companions that lead to the unconscious, benevolent messengers who can take us to new places. They are friendly, and they are able to communicate with us. They can take us to places where we are fearful. Clients often report they become eagles, falcons, or hawks. Bears come up when invoking power, strength, or the fierce mother energy. Others are whales, mice, foxes, and otters.

Humankind has not woven the web of life. We are but one thread within it. Whatever we do to the web, we do to ourselves. All things are bound together. All things connect.

—Chief Seattle, Native American, leader of the Suquamish tribe, peacemaker

Your Totem Animal

In many Native American cultures, young men would go on a quest for their spiritual totem animal. This was a coming-of-age ritual in which the young man would align with the spirit of that animal. They would be forever linked. The young man would travel into the wilderness where he would immerse himself for days, sometimes fasting, sometimes not. By creating stillness and simplicity, he would intensify his focus. Yet with his mind and body clear, he was very active, walking through the forest or mountains with open watchfulness.

By aligning with an animal spirit, we, too, can tap into the power of that animal. It may be the keen eyesight of an eagle that sharpens your awareness of yourself as a great seer. Or it may be the strength of the bear that summons fortitude. It can be a small animal—a minnow or a moth or a lizard.

Empowerment Exercise: Invoking Your Animal Totem

Oftentimes people begin a massage session to invoke their animal spirit with a preconceived notion of the animal they would like to be. Sometimes this is more wish than intuitive information, in Erica's experience. Yet she tells clients to begin with the image of that animal. Sometime during the massage it shifts to another animal. So don't be surprised if another animal pops up.

Because many people like to start out as an eagle, we will use that image for this exercise. This is an exercise that particularly lends itself to music, so if you have something that evokes the eagle, by all means, play it. You will start out face down, and your massage partner will give you a back massage, rubbing the muscles of your shoulders and arms—your wings. Envision the eagle inside you.

Let yourself be engulfed in the massage. Allow yourself to go deeper. Imagine yourself moving into your primal self. Call forth your totem animal by saying, "I invite in the animal spirit of my essence." Allow a scenario to play out in your mind. See the story that you conjure in your mind. If another animal comes forward, switch your awareness to that animal.

A Simple Quest

Follow the massage with this exercise for a richer experience. You may want to do this in conjunction with a series of massages over a week to two weeks to invoke a stronger spirit of your animal totem. Take a day when you can go to a natural area—a river, a forest, a lake, or a mountaintop. Set aside about an hour. (Make sure you dress in layers of comfortable clothing and bring sunscreen and water.) You may want to bring an old blanket to sit on. As you explore the area, bring yourself into mindfulness with your breathing. Store in you the calmness with each breath and ask that the spot where you must stop be revealed to you. When it feels like the right spot, settle yourself in. Close your eyes, and take three deep breaths. Say, "I invite my totem animal, my ally in the spiritual world. Let us find each other."

When you open your eyes, you will want to cultivate calm alertness. You are watchful but not vigilant. You are aware but not engaged. Your mind is not active with thoughts but rather letting them exist. It is still. When thoughts come about what you are seeing, hearing and smelling around you, take it in with respect and awe. Say, "I honor the breeze in the trees that I am hearing now. I am reverent." But then let it go. Let the thought pass. Breathe.

After a time, animals may come into your realm: birds, squirrels, beetles, rabbits, butterflies. When an animal comes into the circle of your awareness, focus on it. Let your spirit speak to it. Imagine your heart opening to it. Notice whether the animal looks at you. Do you make eye contact? Does it speak, as the hawk flying above, to let others know you are there? Does the bird chirp, sending its signal through the woods? If you make eye contact for just a split-second, what is the message you feel coming to you from the animal?

The first time you do this, you may immediately feel chosen by an animal. But if you don't, don't force it. It may take some time to get comfortable feeling a part of the natural world. Let intuition be your guide, and allow yourself to cultivate that intuition on your own timetable. Your intuition will inform you when you have connected with the right spirit animal.

Ray of Light: Hawk Vision

Carolyn has a friend who connected with the hawk as her spirit animal during her pregnancy. This friend had had two miscarriages and undergone a few rounds of fertility treatments before conceiving naturally on what her friend refers to as the fifteenth egg. Because of her struggle, though, Carolyn's friend needed reassurance throughout her pregnancy that the spirit that was coming into the world through her body would get here healthy and sound. On one such day, the friend went hiking in the mountains, asking for that reassurance. That day, a hawk came and landed on a fence post near her. She knew it was the animal spirit linked to her soon-to-be-born son. The hawk reappeared every few days in her last days before delivery.

Empowerment Exercise: Fly Like an Eagle

While you may have chosen another animal spirit, we'd like to turn to the eagle for this exercise because the eagle represents reaching your highest potential. This yoga pose is one of the tougher balancing postures, but if you stay focused and breathe through it, you can do it with practice.

Stand, back straight, feet together. Cross your left arm under your right. Bend both elbows. Twist your hands so your palms are facing. Bring your hands to your face, aligning with your nose. Bend both knees slightly. Let your gaze fall to a spot on the floor a few feet in front of you. Slowly cross your left leg over your right thigh. If you can, wrap your left foot around your right ankle or calf. Breathe through it to settle into a balance. Bend your right knee a little more, keeping your spine straight and hips forward. Breathe and hold it for 10 to 15 seconds.

Bend forward, rounding your back. You are the eagle at rest.

Straighten your torso. Release your left leg and your arms. Hold your leg out to the side and extend your arms. You are a soaring eagle.

Release and reverse the pose, crossing your right arm under the left and your right leg over your left. Release and soar.

Release into soaring eagle.

The Old You

So far, we have connected you with the animal spirit who may have been your kindred spirit for most of your years on the planet. And we have introduced you to animals that help you to identify your potential— where you are going. Part of working through pain and moving forward is creating the capacity to look back without fear and with acceptance. When you can stand and look your old self in the eye without shame or fear, you have become integrated. You are whole.

Real development is not leaving things behind, as on a road, but drawing life from them, as from a root.
—G. K. Chesterton, English poet, novelist, and critic

Stalking New Territory: Grounding

When you work through acceptance using massage, you may find you are in new territory. The key to facing uncertainty is to be grounded. Like the kite in Chapter 5, you soar high but you are tethered to the earth. It often happens when people are experiencing personal growth that they distance themselves from the self they were before. This happens quite a bit when people are working through old emotional pain and they examine their relationships with their parents. In creating the new self who thinks and behaves differently from the messages received in childhood, many people distance themselves from that small child. In shedding themselves of beliefs that no longer serve, they fail to take the step of honoring the experience that led them to that growth. This has the effect of leaving someone feeling untethered.

Take a few moments to write in your Empowerment Journal about your origins. Look, really look, at what has shaped you. Describe your ethnic heritage. Describe your genetic history. If you had some interesting characters in your family lineage, like a tobacco-chewing grandma in combat boots or a fedora-sporting gangster in pinstripes, make a note of them. If you come from a line of hearty old souls, note that. If men in your family die young but women live long healthy lives—or vice versa—note that. In your ethnic lineage, there may be strains of oppression if you are African American, Irish, Jewish, Polish, Croatian, Chinese, Native American, and so on. That's true for so many of us, and you may have inherited more than one strain. Focus not on being the descendent of a victim, but rather on being the descendent of someone who knows the value of compassion and cherishes freedom.

Now make some notes about the place you came from and how it shaped you. What are the values in that place? What are the expected roles for women? For men? What is considered successful? What is deemed noble? What kind of architecture dominates that place? Think of a tree or flower that defines that place. Is there a scent that always brings you back? If you no longer live there, what led you to leave? What might bring you back, and how would you feel about it?

Make some notes about the emotional legacy in your family. What ideas and beliefs did your parents instill in you? Was education valued? Was respect? Honesty? Creative expression? Was there a strong work ethic? Was there unity, a working together for the good of the whole, or was there a lot of competitiveness? Was that competitiveness channeled in a positive way, or was it destructive? Was anger feared, or was it no-holds barred in your family? What weaknesses of your parents did you turn into strengths?

Carolyn has worked for an editor who is known for his eloquence and compassion. He cares not just about getting good stories in the newspaper but about how his writers feel about their work. He wants them to like their work and like working for him. This has become his trademark. Carolyn was surprised to learn that his father was a very cold, distant man who rarely expressed any warmth. This editor clearly had made the choice that he was going to be the one who would check in with how everyone else was feeling. The lesson: We may struggle against our parents' perceived weaknesses, but the gift of that struggle is that we turn them into personal strengths.

Once you've made your notes, distill them down to seven or eight central statements about your origin. Take them beyond the factual to the deep meaning. In other words, don't just say, "I'm African American." Instead, say what that means for who you are for example, "I am African American. Out of that legacy, I have inherited compassion."

Go through the list and honor those gifts. You must bless them, even the ones that have been a struggle for you. It might be, "I come from a family of disunity, and that has made me a strong, self-contained person." You may not yet have mastered a unified family in your adult life. It may be an ongoing process, and it may bring you sadness that you have this yet to overcome. What is important is that you acknowledge that out of that emotional legacy, you became something very, very fine.

Think of this as your values list. It is also your survival list. This is what you have walked through. Out of it, you have formed core values that guide you. These values are your anchor.

Once you walk through your list with your partner, you are ready to be grounded. That you can now honor parts of yourself that you have denied means that you are integrated. This is what anchors you and gives you the capacity to change. It gives you a core so that when uncertainty swirls around you, when you experience the tumult of great change, you are not shaken up. Take from the past what has value for you. The core remains intact; the edges fall away.

Empowerment Exercise: Sealed to Your Self

Use this massage exercise to seal yourself to your beautiful past. The receiving partner lies prone, and the giving partner stands on the right side of the table. Take the receiving partner's right arm and extend it back as far as it will go, resting it palm down on her buttocks. Place your left hand over the last two fingers and the top of her hand. Gently seal it to the gluteal muscle. You are like the glue.

Rest your the heel of your right hand at the base of her spine on the right side with about a half-inch between the spine and the palm of your hand. So your left hand is on her buttocks at the point before the muscle ends at the sacrum. This, too, is a polarity exercise.

Using your left hand, rock the hip. Use your right hand pressing up the spine like it is the fret of a guitar. Press, rock, press, rock, press, rock. Ultimately your right hand ends up at the neck. Your left hand is still gluing her hand down. You can gradually speed this up, moving up, then down the spine.

End with your right hand where it began. Repeat on the other side. Balance with the same kind of rhythm. End with a still hold.

What Is Your Purpose?

The mix of you—as you are here and now—is like none other. You are a snowflake, a matrix of a thousand tiny ice crystals. You are intricately beautiful. You are here for a purpose. You are called to use the painful experiences to hone yourself—physically, emotionally, and spiritually— to achieve that purpose. To *be* that purpose.

Touchstone: The Big Question

Begin this energy massage sitting face-to-face with your partner, cross-legged on the floor. Cover his ears with your hands as he covers your ears with hands. Hold that for a few moments. Let your hands slide down so that you are holding hands. Take his left hand and put it over your heart. Allow him to take your left hand and hold it over his heart. Your hands are still joined.

Now with your faces about 18 inches apart, look into each other's eyes. Hold your partner's gaze. As you do, take in every part of your partner's face with intent mindfulness. Open up your heart and your mind to taking it all in. When you have held your partner's gaze through three deep breaths, move your focus to what you see. Let your eyes take in his forehead, his eyes, his temples, his cheeks, his nose, the creases on his mouth, his lips, the shape of his jaw line, and so on. Spend about 30 seconds on each area, and gently move on to the next area. As your awareness deepens, take in the movements of his face. Though he is holding it still, holding your gaze, notice the movement of a living, breathing spirit. Notice the brightness in his eyes, the blink of an eyelid, the slight crinkle of a smile at the corners of his eyes. Notice his nostrils flare as he breathes in. Share in his aliveness. Acknowledge his life force. Celebrate it. Dive in. Join.

The hardest part of this exercise is holding your partner's gaze. It is hard to let someone hold you, with his awareness of your existence reflected in your eyes. You may feel fear rise up in you as you do. Note the fear. Note the form it takes in your thoughts. As you observe your thoughts, continue to hold his gaze and breathe. Those fear thoughts will grow quiet after a while. You will likely start to feel the safety of another. More than likely, you will also feel it when his fear softens and he begins to feel safe. As you are watching and merging into this other person through his eyes, and he is merging with you through your eyes, and you start to hear the judgment or false findings come up, say "Thank you." Acknowledge and dismiss them. If you can feel the safety in yourself, you can see the safety in another.

Afterward, both of you should share what you felt through the exercise. When did you feel acceptance? When did you feel safe? When the fears came up, what form did the thoughts take? If it didn't come up as a fully articulated thought, where did you feel it in the body, and how did it feel?

After that discussion, you and your partner should ask yourselves honestly, "What is my purpose?" Tell your partner what you think it is. Listen to him relay his question and tell you why. You may want to record all of these thoughts in your Empowerment Journal.

Right Before Your Eyes

It is hard to accept the gaze of a loving other when we aren't sure yet we deserve unconditional acceptance. Yet your one true purpose can be right in front of your eyes. Why do you not yet reach for it? It is just too glorious. It may not be true. You may not deserve it. In using massage to work through acceptance, you can begin to accept that you deserve the richness life wants to offer you.

Chapter 11

Opening to Intimacy

When we open ourselves to love, we enter the kingdom—that is, the realm that we call bliss, the state of not-needing, not-wanting, not-seeking, of complete peace and joy. Some call it heaven. Some call it nirvana. Some call it the lotus circle. Some call it ecstasy.

What is the role of another person in healing? Love heals. It empowers. It educates. It transforms. Only through intimacy can we achieve our deepest knowing. When we unite with another, we achieve a level of intimacy that allows our hearts to open to a much richer experience. We all have a deep desire to return to the Divine, to see His face, to know Her, to be totally merged. Through the other, we can know the Divine. Through the other, we see what is to be exalted in ourselves. We see the way back to love, and only love. We see we are already there.

In this chapter, we will use new age massage techniques to guide you in opening to that intimacy with another that transforms. We will walk you through massage exercises to open your capacity for allowance (root chakra) and allegiance (sexual chakra); we will work with balancing your masculine and feminine energies. While this chapter is not intended to be about sensual massage, we will help you enhance your experience of the sensual to foster deeper awareness of the power of emotional and spiritual intimacy. We also will introduce you to Tantric massage and encourage you to experiment with its principles beyond this book.

The Power of Merging

Love is the glue that bonds us to each other. It allows us to see perfection—in the other person and in ourselves. It allows us to see the pure vitality in another. It revitalizes us. In truth, there is nothing like the "love hit." When you experience it, you glow. You have a sparkle in your eyes. You draw others to you.

While love transforms our hearts and minds, sex is the balm that soothes the soul. Sex softens everything. It makes us melt. We allow ourselves to become vulnerable. We realize we are safe and move out of our defenses. We allow ourselves to feel what we have been blocking out. Through the dance of giving and receiving that is lovemaking, we surge toward completeness. The arrival of the merge—that moment of merging—causes the relaxation. Ah, we have made it through all the defenses, through all the givings and takings, through together-alone, alone-together. The dance of intimacy and individuality is complete.

As you'll remember from Chapter 4, the root chakra is called the allowance chakra, while the sexual chakra is called allegiance. The first step toward intimacy is becoming clear on what we will allow. The "love hit" draws others to us because we are showing to the world that we are allowing possibilities in our lives. We stop drawing others to us when we armor ourselves. We are contracted, so nothing moves.

But the power of allegiance in the sexual chakra is a reminder that it is about choice. We can decide *who* we will align with. We can choose to merge—or not to merge. We can heal our bodies, our minds, our spirits so we make good choices about who to merge with. We can cultivate our awareness so that we know when we are not merging, when we do not accept the other, when we are shutting it out so that it won't even come.

Exempt no one from your love.
—From *A Course in Miracles*

Merging: Relinquishing Judgment

If intimacy is so wondrous, why is it often so difficult? Why do we see articles like life coach Martha Beck's column in *The Oprah Magazine* titled, "Every Little Thing He Does Is Stupid?" In that clever piece, she gives advice on what to do when you are at the point of saying, "Sometimes I just hate him/her."

Intimacy with another, as with self, requires us to let down our defenses, to relinquish our judgments about the other. Really, we think the judgments are about the other, but they very often are about ourselves. They are often about what we fear we are. When we see it in another, we want to ... well, *run!*

Ray of Light: Becoming One

Erica has a client named Jay who has become one of her closest friends. Jay has Lou Gehrig's disease, and while he first came to her nine years ago for massage, he now can only periodically have massage on his feet and hands. He is an inspiration to her because through his dying process, he has achieved a wisdom that transforms his experience to a living process. He is full of light.

Recently, Erica came to his house to give him a foot massage. Jay has a woman who helps him during the day, and this time she asked Erica if she would show her how to give Jay a foot massage. Erica massaged one foot, while the woman massaged the other. But Jay gave the feedback that they weren't the same. The woman was trying to match Erica stroke for stroke. Erica debated about how to coach her and finally came up with this: "It's life. It's not something you're doing to his feet. It's a merging, a joining with him. So it isn't that you envision your hands on his skin, you merge with Jay to his feet." The woman said right away, "Yes, it's about union. It's about becoming one."

The woman immediately recognized her resistance to becoming one with Jay. It meant examining her fears about death and disease. It meant pushing past the resistance to merge with someone or something that is vulnerable, that is less than strong, less than vital—and about allowing *herself* to be vulnerable. And going deeper into the truth, it meant encountering a resistance to Jay's incredible strength and love. We tell ourselves it's about fear of frailty in another. But that's a shield to protect us from illuminating our own inadequacy in the pure light of Jay's capacity for expanding living in the face of dying, to be still and face the truth.

When we merge with someone, we must confront the fear that something we perceive in that person will overwhelm or diminish us. We must confront our judgments and bring them to understanding. We must know we are safe—that the merging of differences only makes both stronger. We must know that when we accept someone as he is, we are accepted and loved for who we truly are. We are giving the same to ourselves.

Empowerment Exercise: The Act of Allowance

Try this energy healing massage with your partner. It is vital that by this point you have a strong foundation of trust between you. You both must feel safe and feel clear about the intention of the massage. This exercise is not sexual. It can be done between two lovers for sexual healing between them, or it can be done between two friends for sexual healing of the individual.

It is crucial throughout this chapter as we explore healing of sexual energy that your intentions are clear. In our culture, we build up many, many layers of misguided beliefs/messages about our sexuality. Sexual energy is power, and when we deal with power, we must deal with our feelings about power over, powerlessness, being victimizer, or victim. They are in our culture, our world; they are in us. This is part of allowance. It is important that both of you feel comfortable with this level of intimacy. Take time to exchange some of your feelings with your massage partner on this subject before moving forward. It is vital that you honor your feelings if the exercises trigger uncomfortable feelings.

Standing on your partner's left side, place both hands on your partner between his pubic bone and belly button. Your hands are side by side. Just stand still, breathe and feel. Notice what it is you feel. Feel your partner's warmth. Feel his pulse. As you continue to breathe, see if you can feel your hands moving into his abdomen. Imagine yourself merging into him. Do you feel the sensation of your hands sinking into his skin? Do not force your way in. Let the receiving partner allow you in.

During your turn as the receiving partner, notice your thoughts and body sensations as you let your partner merge into you. Notice what is happening in your body when your resistance drops.

Complete it by leaving your left hand on the belly. Take your right hand and reach down to the inside of your partner's left leg. Gently brush energy up on inside of leg, up to thighs, to hip, in a horseshoe. Shoot the energy down and off the outside of leg.

> If there isn't fire, then it isn't love. … If it doesn't insist that you move to your next level, if it doesn't take your heart and make it explode in a million pieces, only to fall back together again in some moment of enlightened understanding, then you haven't really loved.
>
> —Marianne Williamson, spiritual teacher and author

Alchemical Marriage

There is a magic inherent in a union of intimacy. There is the sense that it is meant to be, that something higher is taking place here. When you open yourself to accepting the alchemy of emotional and spiritual intimacy, when you allow its power to work in your life, your meetings with others are quite simply enchanted. There are some people when we meet them, we know they are more than just a man or a woman—a lover, a mate, a companion, a partner. There is the sense that the two of you are beyond those roles, that whatever is to happen between you is greater than that. You vibrate the same. You may have a sense of knowingness between you that is always there. You may not yet be in those roles—and you may not ever be—but you *know*. You are linked beyond the external forms your lives may take. Between the two of you, there is a sense of recognition, perhaps still unspoken, that the dance you will do together will be beyond any other partnership you have had with another person. You may have a sense of timelessness about it. You may have just met but sense that you already have known each other for eons. You may have already met his or her energy. You may think, "Oh, yes, that's who he/she is."

When you meet *this* kind of someone, you are ready to drop the veils. The desire to join transcends all—the inner struggle between merging and individuating. You are infinitely willing to deal with the differences between you.

But leading up to that time, your mission is to practice opening, using massage to resolve that inner struggle between the desire for me and the desire for we. Allow yourself to know what it feels like to be open and wanting. Allow life's experiences to chip away at your armor. Let the hurt signal you to go inside and see what part of you is being chipped away, to see what aspect of you is being asked to be changed, to be better.

Empowerment Exercise: Dropping the Veils

In this gentle massage exercise, we will continue the previous exercise, focusing on healing the sexual chakra. The giving partner places both hands on the receiving partner's abdomen. As the receiving partner, notice your resistance. Breathe. As the giving partner, notice when you sense your hands move into your partner. You may notice your partner will sigh and go into a deeper state of relaxation. She may grow still. But also don't be surprised if she begins to twitch, as though an electrical charge is moving through her. This often happens when something has been out of balance and is moving back into balance. Energy is being released.

When you sense the energy being released, move to the head. Using both hands, hold your thumbs above her head, a few inches away. You should feel a warmth coming from her head. Stretch your hands out so that each little finger (Earth element) is pointing to an ear. Say, "Earth," placing your little fingers at her ears. Next place your ring fingers (water element) on her temples. Say, "Water." As you lay the middle fingers down, say, "Fire." As you lay the pointer fingers down, say, "Air." Touch the thumbs to her scalp, saying, "Ether." Your hands are gently cupping these energy pathways. Focus allowing your fingers to merge into her head. Hold for one to two minutes.

To conclude, move to her feet. Put your hands under her ankles. Hold them until you feel your partner move into deeper relaxation, or something jerks or twitches. Swoosh your hand in a gentle horseshoe motion, similar to the previous exercise. Move with a Divine energy between her legs, out to her hips, pulling the energy down the outside of the legs. End on that.

Done correctly, this exercise moves you into a higher level because you are moving into the same energy that allows us to do craniosacral work, the deepest level at which you can touch the body physically. Don't be surprised if when you are holding your partner's ankles you feel a deep movement in the body—a deeper pulse. You are getting to the essence. The veils have dropped. This is the life force. This is all there is and all that matters.

> The smoke of my own breath,
> Echoes, ripples and buzz'd whispers … love-root, silk-thread, crotch and vine,
> My respiration and inspiration. … the beating of my heart. … the passing of blood and air through my lungs,
> The sniff of green leaves and dry leaves, and of the shore and dark-color'd sea-rocks, and of hay in the barn.
> —Walt Whitman, from "Song of Myself" in *Leaves of Grass*

Hold your partner's essence in your hands.

From Therapeutic to Sensual

When we shift from therapeutic massage to sensual massage, we leave behind technique. It's not about how you manipulate the muscles and tissue. It's about exploring. Allow yourself to play, to experience pleasure, to receive as well as give. Allow yourself to fully experience the sensation of touch. In other words, don't think so much.

Touchstone: The Aromatic

Your assignment is to go with your partner to a bath and body store with a wide selection of aromatic lotions and oils. Test all the testers. Share your favorite scents. Place the oil on his wrist. Let him rub the lotion into your hands. Make it game. Explore.

Back at home, having chosen a lotion or oil you both like, take a few moments simply to experience the sensation of the warm oil. Pour a little into the palm of your hand. Swirl one palm over the other, clockwise. Move one palm back and forth over the top of your hand. Sweep your oiled hand out over the forefinger. Do this for three strokes. Slowly do the same with each finger, repeating for three times. Sweep your hand forward over the top of your other hand, moving toward the heart, up the wrists. Take delight in the pleasure of the oil on your hands. Switch hands.

Try the same with your partner, smoothing the oil on his hands.

The Kundalini Way: Awakening to Sensual Massage

When our sensual feelings lie dormant, we come to the point of not trusting our own feelings. We don't trust that our own body sensations are pleasurable—or we don't even notice them. As you are giving massage, you may be hesitant that you are not doing it right. Trust the information that is coming to you. Tune in to the way the oil feels on your hands. Tune in to the feel of her skin. Notice when it feels as though you are sinking into him. Notice when there is resistance. Hold it there, breathe and notice when it drops. Notice what is happening in your own body when you feel the resistance drop—a lift, a tingle, a general sense of contentment. If it feels good to you as the giving partner, it feels good to the receiving partner.

Try a backrub, with your partner lying prone. Use music, something that evokes the water element—strings, piano, something instrumental with a lot of flow and not a lot of percussion. Place your hand in small of her back. Start rocking her hips, like you are rocking a baby. Do the same horseshoe-shape swoosh stroke from inner thigh and out. Move to kneading buttocks in slow, steady, deep strokes. Elongate movement up the spine. Move upward, from base of spine to head. This movement activates the kundalini energy along the spine.

Kundalini energy is the latent cosmic energy force—the origin of all your power, all your strength and all forms of life you may assume. As Kundalini energy rises in the body, it encounters blocks in the form of muscles and tissue that are armored with tension. It is often described as working like an electrical current. The friction caused by the resistance of the armoring to the rising energy produces heat, and this burns away the tension, cleansing and purifying the channels. The result is a freer flow of energy.

As you receive a Kundalini backrub, notice the streaming sensation of the freed energy. Feel it flow through your genitals, your belly and your heart. With each stroke, feel yourself expand. Imagine the undercurrent of the ocean taking you beyond the boundaries of your physical body. It is an intense sensation of joy, of being elevated, of being relaxed.

Empowerment Exercise: The Awakening

This massage stimulates and relaxes the intestines, which are the emotional center in the body, and opens the sexual chakra. Begin by rubbing warm oil on your hands, with your partner lying on his back. Rub your hands on his abdomen, moving clockwise. (We always move clockwise in the abdomen because that's the way the intestines flow.)

Stand on the left side of the table. Place your left hand under your partner's neck and your right hand below the belly button. Use the oil generously on your hands. Put both hands together on his belly, moving gently. Remind him to keep breathing just before you touch his belly. Move in a swishing circular motion, like you are working with clay.

Move your hands to cup the sides of his body. With alternating hands, gently pull his torso up about an inch from the table. Your fingertips will touch the back of his body. Do this with gentle pressure all the way up to his armpits. Because the sides of the body rarely get touched, this is a very comforting touch. This is where the lymph system resides, too, so stimulation and relaxation allow the body to cleanse itself.

Adding more oil if necessary, sweep your left hand up from his belly, up the sternum, first to the left shoulder and out his arm, then repeat with the right hand, sweeping up and out the shoulder and the arm.

Positioning yourself next to his hips, place flat open hands on his abdomen, with the bottom edge of your hands next to his pubic bone, your fingers pointed toward his head. Slide your hands in a straight line up the middle of his body. As he in inhales, you prepare. As he exhales, push deeply through the abdomen, moving to the rib cage. When he completely empties of breath, stop your hands. He inhales again, and on the exhale, move again. Repeat this until you reach the bottom of his rib cage. Do this with deep breathing several times. Return to circular motions on the abdomen. Move your left hand to the sternum. Your left hand holds his heart. Your right is below his belly button, over his sexual chakra. End on that connection.

For nothing is fixed, forever and forever and forever, it is not fixed; the earth is always shifting, the light is always changing, the sea does not cease to grind down rock. Generations do not cease to be born, and we are responsible to them because we are the only witnesses they have. The sea rises, the light fails, lovers cling to each other, and children cling to us. The moment we cease to hold each other, the sea engulfs us and the light goes out.

—James Baldwin, American writer

Mirror, Mirror

When we are first attracted to someone, we see in that person the glorious. It is intoxicating. We are drawn to that person. We only want to get closer. We cannot get enough of that person. The desire to unite, to merge with someone, the magnificence of discovery is the enchanted journey toward the Beloved. What we receive back from that person is the mirror image of the Divine. Through love's eyes we see the Divine in that person, and reflected back in the mirror is the splendor of ourselves.

That's why intimacy is just as much a dance with the self as with the other. As we work within the relationship, the mirror of the relationship reflects those places within us that are calling out for healing, for balance. We love, we are vulnerable, we feel safe, we drop the veils, we see what we need to see. Through love we can allow it to happen. So the next step, after dropping the veils, is to drop the scales from our eyes. We are no longer blind. The other person reflects to us what we need to see and to know.

The art of mirroring is discerning in the other what part is ourselves being reflected. Your duty to yourself—and your intimate partner—is to take responsibility for the fears and protections and antiquated belief systems that are revealed to you in the mirror of the other.

A true loving relationship *should* push the boundaries. If it's not, you may be hiding behind the mask of intimacy. So this law of mirroring is as it should be. This is why people come together. The body does build up armoring over time, and much of this armoring is in the genital area. The experience of intimacy is so closely intertwined with our desire for security that often armoring takes place in the body in the root and sexual chakras, which is why we have worked thus far with those two chakras. You can use massage exercises to bolster your commitment to taking responsibility for what you see in the mirror of the relationship. This can be done simply by preparing for a massage session with your partner that invokes that intention. Ask that those energies in you that have not been expressed—the shadow side—come forth.

Map of the Heart

In your Empowerment Journal, write about relationships you may have had that tested the limits of intimacy—that showed you information about yourself you weren't ready to know. How did you respond to that information? What fears did it bring up? What beliefs formed around that? Make a list. Are those beliefs really true? Challenge yourself. Share with your partner as much of this as you feel comfortable with. Commit to challenging each other about old patterns and antiquated beliefs.

Uniting of Masculine and Feminine Energies

Intimacy happens. It is inevitable. It's about completion, about being whole. It's above and beyond the biological urge of the species to reproduce itself. It's about a deep yearning to express wholeness. There is a lot of talk, especially for women, in this culture advising us not to believe that we are "half" or "less than" if we are not mated, and we don't mean to imply that you are incomplete if you are not in an intimate partnership at the moment. We certainly understand the value of being alone is just as important in cultivating our capacity for intimacy. Being comfortable with our aloneness is vital to our ability to be part of two. Some people experience tremendous growth during forced—or chosen—times of celibacy. Others *avoid* growth by diving into intimacy—or the illusion of intimacy.

What we do mean about wholeness is more along the lines of "no man is an island." There are parts of ourselves yearning to be expressed that are only expressed in relationships. Trust us, even if you don't have an intimate partnership, you have relationships in your life that are for the spiritual purpose of growth. *All* relationships do this; all relationships should be intimate. So, spiritually, you don't get off the hook. It isn't time out. It's never time out.

When we come into this world, we manifest as a male or female expression, and we are commissioned from the start with a lifetime assignment: Cultivate the other energy. We are in some ways divided. Parts of us may remain unexpressed until we experience growth or until we unite with the opposite energy (masculine or feminine). This is true even in same-sex relationships. On some level, the union occurs for both partners to open to expressing more of the energy that is least natural to them. Ultimately, it is built into the design of the Universe that through the struggle of differences with others, you can become whole within yourself.

Sun and Moon Meditation

You may use this meditation in conjunction with a massage session to unite your masculine and feminine energies, harnessing the masculine energy of the sun and the feminine energy of the moon. The energies of the sun and moon meet at that slice of the day when the sun is setting in the west and the moon is rising in the east. Use this meditation to help you expand into that sacred space of the day. Start with three calming deep breaths. Face east. Inhale and say, "I welcome you, Mother Moon." Visualize the pearlescent reflection of the moon. Visualize its energy flowing from the eastern horizon to your heart. Now turn west. Inhale and say, "I welcome you, Father Sun." Visualize the golden blaze of the sun. Visualize its energy flowing from the western horizon to your heart. Inhale and say, "Meet in me." Exhale and say, "Flow in me." Repeat several times, visualizing the two energies flowing into the other within the circle-space of your heart.

Loving and Losing

There are many reasons we fail to open our hearts completely to the full range of experience intimacy offers. We may have stored in our bodies the pain of past relationships, or we may simply have blunted our experience of the sensual, choosing to dwell in the world of words and ideas, commerce and money, choosing to shut out the emotion.

But remember, there is no way to love and lose. There is only love. You don't have to turn the love off, even if you have to break away from the loved one. The love still exists. The loving truth is that the relationship is no longer what it was.

A spiritual teacher of *A Course in Miracles* once spoke about the way of remaining open to love yet protected from those who would harm our hearts. The path: radiate. It seems paradoxical to be so wide open when our instinct is to protect, to close off. But your protection is that you will *only* radiate your allegiance to yourself and your path. You will only radiate love, truth, kindness, grace, and clarity. When you are *only* aligned with Perfect Love, in the form of the Divine, you will *only* draw to you those who are on your level of enlightenment. It's like a brilliant white floodlight. It's blinding. It's disorienting. But it is only so to those who are not yet ready for what you are ready for. The white light will turn them away. It will shine on the darkness the others don't want to see. It may dazzle those who would seek you at first. But quickly it will be apparent whether they are ready to approach the light.

This series of exercises leading up to a massage session can guide you in radiating, drawing to you the emotional and spiritual intimacy that transcends.

Step One: Radiant Heat

For this meditation, you will use a deep red candle. Have fun with it, choosing a scent, shade, and texture that enlivens your imagination: orchard red, cranberry, cinnamon burberry. The red symbolizes your root chakra. It signals that you are secure and intact. It symbolizes your capacity for allowance.

Sit comfortably, cross-legged on a pillow in front of the burning candle. As you gaze into the flame, repeat the following. After each statement, breathe in and out three times. Let the words sink in. Imagine your words, your breath, your intention settling in your root chakra. Imagine that you are creating a reservoir of deep knowing.

I am love. I am only love.
I am kindness. I am only kindness.
I am compassion. I am only compassion.

I am truth. I am only truth.
I am safe. I am only safe.
I am safety. I am only safety.
I am alive. I am only alive.
I am strength. I am only strength.
I am courage. I am only courage.
I am knowing. I am only knowing.
I am life. I am only life.

With each statement, focus on the glow of the flame. Imagine storing the flame within you. Imagine it burning brightly within.

Step Two: Camel Pose

This yoga pose releases your heart chakra, while activating your root and sexual chakras. Kneel with your legs hip-width apart. Place your hands on your lower back, fingers pointing down. Slide your hips forward as though they are pressed against an imaginary wall. Lifting from the chest, slowly bend your torso back, sliding your hands down your buttocks and backs of your legs until you can grab each ankle. Slowly move your hands onto your heels. Take a deep breath. Exhale, pressing the front of your thighs, hips, and abdomen forward. Hold for 5 to 10 seconds.

Open your heart.

Step Three: Purifying Massage

Use this breath awareness massage to purify when an old relationship is lingering and you want to clear it out and open space for something new. The role breath plays in this is by releasing the carbon dioxide in your lungs; you are releasing that depleted air.

Before you start, take some time to look at the past relationship. Surrender what you could not change. Accept that person as she was. Examine what you received from the relationship. How did it make you a better person? What was the value of the relationship?

As you receive this massage from your partner, direct your breath to your sexual and root chakras. Breathe deep down into your root chakra. This is the piece that allows you to release your past. When that feels complete, direct your breath to your sexual chakra. This is the piece that is about your next step. This is about your choices. Ask for that to be opened for you.

This massage focuses on the legs. Your thighs hold sexual energy. As the giving partner with the receiving partner lying on her back, begin with a long sweeping movement from the ankles, over the knees, up to the pelvis. As you reach the pelvis, move your hands to her backside, slipping under her lower back, over her kidneys. Move your hands down to her buttocks. You should be able to feel her sacrum. With one hand, push your fingers into her buttocks muscles, rocking her with your other hand, opening her leg out.

Pull your hand out, sweeping up her legs again, getting underneath as much as you can. With your hands horizontally across her thigh, your fingers on her inner thigh, pull out, using deep pressure. This is a kneading motion, with fingers and palms. It's like you are pulling the flesh away from the bone. Do this, moving from the top of the thigh to the knee. Now move vertically from the knee going up the thigh, with one stroke knee to hip, the other ankle to hip.

At her ankles, cup two hands with your right hand underneath, fingers on the outside and thumb on the inside, and with your left hand cupped above, fingers on the inside, thumb on the outside, so that her ankle is encircled. Use the weight of your body to press into her calves, in a deep movement up to her knee. At the knee, pull back your weight, resuming deep pressure after you pass her knee, moving up her thigh. Mold your hands around her thigh bone. Push up to the hip, stopping your hands on her inner thigh before coming to the groin. Sweep your hands to the outside of her legs, using slight pressure all the way down her outer and inner thighs.

The Tantric Way

Many of the steps we have already taken in this chapter lay the groundwork for exploring Tantric massage. We have worked to awaken you to the sensations of your body, to show you that the first step to pleasure lies in your appreciation of yourself. Trust is a vital step, as is activating your sense of play. By harmonizing your masculine and feminine energies, you are no longer bound to gender roles in sexuality, and you become more open to adventure during an erotic experience.

Tantra is an Eastern science of spirituality that includes sexuality as a doorway to ecstasy and enlightenment. It originated in India in 5000 B.C.E. through the cult of the Hindu god Shiva and his consort, the goddess Shakti. Shiva is believed to be the embodiment of pure consciousness in its most ecstatic state, while Shakti is believed to be the embodiment of pure energy. Hindus believe that in uniting sexually and spiritually with Shiva, Shakti gave form to his spirit and created the universe.

In the Tantric belief system, the creation of the world, then, is an act of erotic love. It sees all living beings as a reflection of the joyful dance between Shiva and Shakti. This erotic dance of life is the root of all existence.

Tantra means "weaving" in Sanskrit. The joyful dance of Tantra is the process of unifying the many paradoxes and complexities of the self into one harmonious whole. It also means "expansion." Once our individual energies are unified, we can expand into joy.

One of the most basic principles in Tantric sex is the prolonging of pleasure in order to experience greater ecstasy. Some of the massage exercises we have used thus far—the awakening and purifying massages—can be used in a sexual context to create the stream of energy that awakens the ecstatic response. By staying relaxed during states of high arousal, you allow orgasmic energy to flow uninterrupted through your body.

This is the miracle that happens every time to those who really love: The more they give, the more they possess.
—Rainer Maria Rilke, Austrian German lyrical poet

Giving and Receiving Pleasure

During lovemaking, you are each fulfilling yourselves—and you do it together. Both are receiving, receiving, receiving. But the most fundamental desire is to receive *yourself*. When you allow yourself to receive, the other begins to receive. It's pleasurable for us when we know someone else is receiving pleasure. There is nothing more titillating than wanting it so much—when you want to receive, when you *demand* it. It's exhilarating that someone could want you that much. It's the feeling of *He has accepted me*. Or *She has taken me in*. The dance of ecstasy is that between the desire for pleasure and the acceptance of pleasure.

To use massage to heighten your capacity for pleasure, we use many of the same techniques that we have used thus far to work through pain. Why? Because pleasure and pain are two sides of a dichotomy. Your work breathing through pain during massage exercises has laid the groundwork for experiencing greater pleasure. (Great! Extra points!) By seeing the pain not as something to club over the head or to conquer, by joining with the pain, you develop a new view pain: It is not the enemy. It may seem almost unfathomable that we could think of pleasure as an enemy, but it is true that though our minds might tell us we want pleasure, there is another part of ourselves that whispers, "But you are not entitled to it. You *can't* allow yourself to feel this good."

Just as we have embraced pain, no longer seeing pain as the enemy, we can embrace pleasure fully. Take the time to choose one of the massage exercises we have already outlined in this chapter, using it to unite with your desire for pleasure. Use your breath throughout to heighten your experience of making friends with pleasure. Direct your breath to your sexual chakra, moving it up and out over your body. Each time you inhale, imagine it like a bucket to a well, drawing water. Let the water-breath flow over your entire body.

From Ecstasy to the Ultimate: Meeting the Divine

Human love as a mirror of Divine love is a strain of thought running through many spiritual belief systems, from Bhatki yoga to Sufism to Christianity. It is believed to be the path to understanding the depth and breadth of God's love for us. In the New Testament, the love of Jesus for his followers is parallel with the love between groom and bride. Followers are described as "the bride of Christ." The church is described as the "body of Christ," united as one in functioning as His purposes. In the Old Testament, the book Song of Solomon is the poetry of love and passion. The song between the two lovers mirrors the ardor of our Creator for us.

So the path to opening to intimacy with another is the path to the ultimate. In the one we love, we meet the Beloved, our Creator, our Source. As we develop a greater emotional intimacy, we deepen our spiritual intimacy. It's a wondrous journey; massage can ease the way.

Chapter 12

Spirit Connections Through Touch

Touch and psychic intuition are intertwined. With the senses of sight and hearing, we can put words to it, use logic, define what we experience in scientific and declarative terms. But there is an element to touch that transcends the words and logic. Touch is magic. Massage is magic, too. This is where psychic intuition comes in.

From the moment you began the journey of this book, no doubt you activated your intuition. If you'll remember at the outset, we described what happens the first time Erica meets a client, the way she gathers information. As you have moved through these exercises, undoubtedly you have sensed the energy moving through your body. And perhaps all along you have sensed there is more than just your body, your mind, and your spirit in the room.

In this chapter, we will explore the role that the realm beyond the material world plays in massage. We will show you how to activate your psychic sense of yourself and your partner. We will connect with the realm of the spirit and gain a more universal perspective of your body and who you are.

How Erica Does It

Erica has been cultivating her psychic intuition in conjunction with massage for 15 years. She sees the first step is in nurturing her capacity for empathy. Then she moves to being observant of the dance between herself, the energy of the body, and the energy of the universe. It's like a water dance. Imagine yourself diving underwater, merging with the deep sea, and that's what it's like. Erica must let go of her boundaries, allow herself to be permeable. She must allow herself to meld into her client and feel what he feels.

The first thing Erica does when she walks into the massage room is touch her client in some way. It's always different, but she lets intuition guide her. Sometimes it comes as a clear thought; sometimes it just comes and she acts. If she is not clear, she takes a deep breath. When the thought comes to just "start anywhere," that's information, too. It indicates to her that the client may have some fear about beginning. She is picking up on anticipatory anxiety.

Erica always starts a session by asking the client to do three exhales. It allows what is internal to become more external. Erica describes it to clients as bringing all the chaos from the inside up and out.

That first touch is the first step to bringing into form the swirling mists of energy in the room. By touching the client, the form of energy becomes clear to Erica. She may recognize it as a pattern. The thought may come, for instance, that "Let's pull this energy down through the left side of body, through the pelvis."

As Erica massages different areas of the body, as the client is breathing through it, they encounter pain together. More and more information is flushed out. With each touch, information rises from the very cells of the person's skin.

Each massage session is like a symphony of many movements. It begins with a prelude, then the energy intensifies, continues to stir, reaches a crescendo. As the energy is resolved, it falls, knitted back together in a new pattern. During your next massage with your partner, imagine the energy of your pain arising from your body, released and realigning, much like a weaving. Once released pain reaches a peak and is resolved, the threads of energy reweave themselves in a new warp and weft, settling into a new pattern. Every session has that flow to it.

The intuitive mind is a sacred gift and the rational mind is a faithful servant.
We have created a society that honors the servant and has forgotten the gift.
—Albert Einstein, German-born American scientist and inventor

The More You Know

Intuition is another way of saying your innate wisdom. The more you practice with intuition, the more you have. Already many of the exercises we have used have put you in training for intuitive touch. When we direct you to use a still hold during a massage, waiting to receive a slow, steady heat from your partner's shoulder or feet, we are training you to tune into your intuition. Remember in Chapter 3 when we talked about hara? Hara is the dance of that energy. You may already have the instinct about the dance of energy, but as you practice, you will gain the tools to articulate how it is you know what you know. The more you know about the source of intuitive touch, the more confident you feel.

Touchstone: Your Psychic Intuition

With your partner, do a simple massage placing yourself in Erica's experience. State, "I am open to whatever information I receive." You may notice your instinct is to humble yourself, to discount the information you receive. You may be afraid if you proceed with the massage—moving to a certain area or lingering in another—based on the information you get that you are doing it wrong or causing harm. Don't limit yourself. Don't judge it. Just say, "This is what I'm receiving." Check it out.

When Erica is giving a massage, she may get information coming in about a client's grandmother. Perhaps the grandmother was a big influence in that person's life. After 15 years of trusting her intuition, Erica knows to go with it. She may ask, "Did you have an extraordinary connection with your grandmother?" She often will find the question breaks through and leads to a greater healing.

Ray of Light: The Angel Who Awaits

During a massage with Rachel, Erica saw Rachel's father come to her in angelic form. She asked Rachel what role her father had played in her life. Rachel had been working out a strained relationship with her mother.

But Erica kept getting a powerful image of Rachel's father. "Where was your father during all this?" Erica asked her. Rachel reacted with stunned silence. Then she said, "My father was always there, just waiting for me. I have always felt my father was holding a space for me."

Erica described the image that came to her of Rachel's father—a strong, wise entity. She described him as an angel. Rachel was intrigued at the appearance of her father in angelic form; she hadn't ever sensed him that way. Rachel fell into silence, and Erica continued with the massage. Suddenly Rachel wept. She confessed that by looking only at her mother's emotional legacy, her mother's lineage was the only line she had ever pursued. In that moment, she realized her true strength derived from the lineage of her father. Over subsequent massage sessions, it became apparent this revelation was pivotal for Rachel. She was able to work through her present-time issue of risking ostracism by speaking the truth. Through accessing the true strength she inherited from her father, she was able to overcome a lifelong mistrust of her intuition.

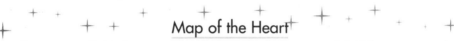

Map of the Heart

Do you recall the first time you learned there were angels? What images of angels surrounded you in your upbringing? As a child, did you believe in angels? Do you still? Do you remember the first time you sensed angels around you—perhaps in a time of great despair or grief, perhaps in a brush with death? Do you have loved ones who have passed on, and have you ever sensed they were sending a message to you? Write about this in your Empowerment Journal.

The Blessing Spirit

Many of Erica's clients have remarked that they felt Erica placed a candle next to their heads on the right side during a massage. She had not. They described it as an intense heat next to their faces and envisioned it as a candle.

Other clients have told Erica they felt as though her hands were in four different places on their bodies. Sometimes Erica was not even touching them at that moment. Or some speak of feeling hands on their bodies they believed were Erica's and in the next moment, they felt Erica's hands touch them in another place on the body. One said he felt Erica's hands on his head at the same time he felt three other sets of hands on him.

Erica experiences many moments when it is as though she and someone else have been working during a massage. Or sometimes she will see an angelic form come into the room. Sometimes she sees guides; sometimes she just senses them.

Massage engenders the receptivity to receiving a blessing spirit from the beyond. Whether it's an angel, the spirit of a loved one who has passed on, or a spirit guide, it most often comes in the form of a message or a benevolent spirit. Sometimes it comes to clients, sometimes to Erica, sometimes to both. Grandmothers come in quite often. Sometimes fathers, sometimes mothers. Sometimes it's the archangel Michael. Sometimes a Buddhalike figure!

The more you allow yourself the possibility of the presence of spirit, the more spirit comes through.

The Third Eye

Typically, to activate psychic abilities, we work with the sixth chakra, or the third eye. It's the energy of knowledge, the place in us where we are receptive to universal wisdom. But for Erica, that is only part of the picture. She found third eye energy came from the masculine way of seeking knowledge—in the same spirit as the Stalking Yourself exercises we have done. She believed the missing component was the receptivity to knowledge, the feminine way of drawing in wisdom. Erica came to this only after trying it solely through her third eye chakra. During that time, she was having intense lower back pain. Every three months or so, she would suffer for about a week and a half. She wouldn't be able to move and would have to stay in bed. Finally she asked her spiritual teacher, "Why does my back hurt so much?" His reply was that she was lifting too much energy out of her back to her third eye, thinking she had to see from there. Her lower back wasn't getting the support it needed. He told her she was letting go of her innate wisdom, which comes from her sexual chakra of allegiance. He advised her to use the lower back pain as a signal to herself that she was seeking and doing in a masculine way at the neglect of her feminine way.

Since then, Erica uses massage to stimulate the third eye chakra and sexual chakra in conjunction with one another. The sexual chakra of allegiance is about being loyal and true to your own path, your own way of doing and seeing.

Empowerment Exercise: Activating Psychic Intuition

As the giving partner, place one hand on her third eye chakra, the other on the sexual chakra, your palm between her belly button and pubic bone. Both of you will breathe deeply, experiencing first the energy of the third eye chakra, then the other. Consciously invite these two energies to unite.

In starting at the head, your intention is to stir up energy, opening the third eye chakra. Stand at your partner's head, placing your fingers lightly on her temples. Notice the muscles above her ears. Move your fingers to both sides of her head. Holding your fingers in place, move your hands, jiggling her head from side to side. You are wiggling the scalp at the same time you are rocking her head back and forth. Gradually increase the movement. Come to her forehead, placing fingers on the third eye, circling clockwise.

Continue finger pressure, moving down the neck and out the shoulders, pressing trigger points.

Using your full hand, do compressions moving down the body, first on the right side, then the left, in slow, deep movements. This stimulates blood flow.

Moving to the second chakra, or sexual chakra, mirror the movements you did at the head. Start with soothing circles on the belly, moving clockwise. Now reach across her body, placing one hand on the pelvic bone. Gently rock the pelvis, gradually increasing the movement. Move to the other side. Repeat. Press trigger points. Palpitate the abdomen. This is assertive movement. It is not meant to be soothing. You are stirring things up.

As the receiving partner, focus your breath on experiencing the energy of allegiance to yourself. Say out loud, "My allegiance is to myself and to my path."

Once the crescendo has passed, move into stillness. Place one hand on your partner's abdomen, over the sexual chakra, and the other hand over the third eye. Hold it as your partner experiences those two energies working together. Say, "Feel my hand. Feel the energy of allegiance. Allow the energy of allegiance to merge with the energy of knowledge. Allow these to co-mingle within you."

As the receiving partner, notice what you see in your mind's eye. Do memories come up? Let whatever might come forward do so. You may experience an intensifying of colors.

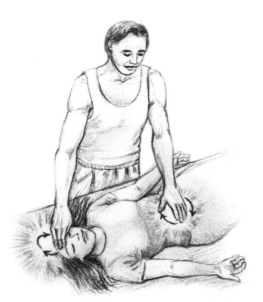

*Activating psychic intuition through the third
eye and sexual chakras.*

An Invitation

Let's say that you would like to bring a family member or other loved
one who has passed on into a massage session. How can you do that?
Open your massage session with an intention. Sometimes Erica does a
prayer or invocation at the outset of a massage. Start your massage session by saying, "Today we are asking to receive further understanding
about the dynamic between (*your name*) and (*person you are calling
forth*). We ask that you come forward to help with this learning."

As the receiving partner, let your memories or images guide you. Share
with your partner what you are seeing and hearing. It may start with the
image of something formless before it comes to you as a person. Sometimes
clients will tell Erica, "Now I see a great big ball of black gunk in my
pelvis. It hurts." Or often clients will get the image of sharp-pointed metal.
Erica will move to that part of the body. If your partner has an image
come up, let that guide you in where you move to massage him and in

the intensity of strokes. Sometimes a client will have an epiphany and may say something like, "Oh, now I understand my father. That's why he was always saying such-and-such." Or they may understand why they responded to that person in a certain way. As you receive massage from your partner, share these insights. Narrate as it transforms. Often after the presence of the person is made known, clients will experience the energy change or take another form. It may be the sensation of fire burning through the body, then it becomes something else. Or they may envision themselves as a seagull and transform to an eagle. These "visits" can be powerful.

Ray of Light: Message from Beyond

Deidre was coming to Erica to use massage to work through horrific abuse she had experienced as a child from her parents. She had committed to using massage to empower herself and no longer be a victim. Every time Deidre came over a six-month period, she would bring someone in through massage, and she would receive an assignment. One time a guide told her the title of a book she had never heard of; she bought it and read it. At the time she was coming to Erica, Deidre's father was dead and her mother still living. She was very distant toward her mother, still struggling to understand her. At the point where she had already done a lot of healing work in massage, she announced at the outset of a massage session that she was ready to manifest her heart's desire in her life. During the session, her father came to apologize to her for the abuse. He explained some of the events so that she understood her mother better. He asked her forgiveness. Shortly after that, Deidre met the man she now lives with.

The Spiritual Connection

Opening yourself to experiences of wisdom from the other side is just the beginning of tapping into a more universal perspective. Massage can open the portal to the vast order of the universe, to your place in it, to your part in the bigger whole. By opening you to that perspective, that of Creator, that of grace, compassion, and wisdom of the ages, you gain infinite peace. You gain connection.

When you were a child, do you remember lying on the summer lawn looking up at the stars? Do you remember that first moment it occurred to you that something was beyond you, your mother and father, your home, your school, your town? Do you remember first asking what might be beyond you? Carolyn often smiles at the openness of her twins, now four, whose perspective is still big enough to include the possibility that we might all live on different planets someday. They haven't drawn a limit on it. They see Earth as just one possibility. Children quite naturally are open to psychic information. They have more willingness to let go of boundaries. To them, it's possible that the grandmother they visit twice a year on the other side of the country might live on another planet. To them, it's possible that someday they will live on the moon. To them, the universe is vast. They accept it when Carolyn tells them she talks to her father every day, though he has been deceased nine years. This is not frightening to them. It's exhilarating. They see their connection to the larger whole. They give themselves permission to be that big.

Massage is a way to experience a deeper awareness with the collective consciousness, to see your slice in this huge thing called life. It's a way to call in this information. Through the massage exercises in this chapter, we will guide you in discovering where you fit in.

Universe Meditation

One of the first steps in tapping into the collective unconscious is to acknowledge the vastness of the universe. Start a massage session with this guided visualization that parallels that childhood moment of first asking the question, that innocent curiosity and openness to all possibilities. One partner should read it aloud to the other.

Lying on your bed at night take in your immediate surroundings— your bed, the lamp, the dresser. (Or if it's summer, go ahead and lie on the lawn. Notice the grass, the roots of trees, the crickets chirping.) Hold that image of you as you move out, above you looking down from the ceiling (or the treetops). Now move higher, above your house. Move out, above your whole neighborhood, imagining the rooftops of all the houses on your street. Stay at each point as long as it takes to pull in the image, not just to see it but to linger in the sounds and movement of the scene. Hear the dogs barking in the yard down the street, hear the couple whispering on the back patio in the dark while their children sleep in the house. Always keep your focal point on you, lying on the bed (or the grass), as you grow smaller and smaller in the picture.

Move out, above your city, hovering over the city lights. Again, linger there, hearing the sirens in the streets, seeing the twinkling lights. Keep your focal point on you, as you become smaller. Move out again, over your state, then higher still, above your country, slipping out beyond the clouds, seeing the sphere that is Earth come into view. Each time, collect a snapshot of you. Move out further still, past the sun, out past Jupiter and the rings of Saturn, to the edge of the solar system. Move out through the Milky Way, through the other galaxies, past red dwarf stars and binary stars and black holes, to the quasars and the edge of the universe. At the edge, imagine that you have met the energy of the Divine, that you have heard His voice and felt his benevolent presence, that you have felt it flowing around you the entire time. Imagine that you have traversed a river, finding the wellspring, its source, that you have known the current of it all along. Imagine that you feel it flowing from every edge of the universe through the quasars, the stars, the other galaxies, the Milky Way, back into our solar system, down to Earth, to your country, your state, your city, your neighborhood, your house—to you.

Take a few moments to record your experience of this meditation in your Empowerment Journal.

Empowerment Exercise: The Sky's the Limit

In this massage exercise, we will be uniting the crown chakra with the feet, balancing the energies of Earth (feet) and heaven (crown chakra). If you'll remember in Chapters 5 and 6 we used a lot of breath work and foot massage, which lay the foundation for the experiences of the sublime. Most of the physical work is done at the feet. But the goal is to move the energy up and out the head. By working the feet, a negative pole, it allows the head to open. This massage is ideally done two on one, with the one person working at the head at the same time another works the feet. The experience of four hands on your body also invokes the blessing spirit to be brought into the room. We will call the massaging partners for this exercise Earth (feet) and heaven (head). It is written as though heaven is a male, Earth is a female and the receiver is a female.

Start by stating the intention: To let yourself expand to the experience of the collective unconscious. Heaven stands at the receiver's head, placing his hands on her crown chakra; Earth stands at her feet. The receiver says, "I am opening to the vast energy of the universe. I want to see myself as part of a larger wholeness."

218

Heaven places his fingertips on the receiver's head. Moving his hands but not his fingers, he wiggles her head from side to side. The goal is to stimulate. He moves from the scalp to the neck, pressing his fingers into the sides of her neck. He rocks her neck from side to side.

As the receiving partner, focus on mushing up your face. Drop your jaw. Wiggle it up and down. You are opening up your facial muscles. You are loosening up, trying to knock yourself out of patterns in your head.

As heaven starts, Earth reaches up under her calves. Her fingertips will just skim the backs of the receiver's knees. Earth works the fine trigger points on the center line of the outer and inner calf, moving in a straight line down to the feet. As she exhales, press. On the inhale, stop, wait. As she exhales, press again. Repeat.

Moving to the feet, Earth places her fingers between the metatarsals, the bones of the feet. She should feel the soft spot between the bones. Starting at the toes, she slides back. The whole top of the foot reflexes to the back of the body, so this stimulates the spine, which opens you to awareness and receptivity to information. Do this slide several times, working each foot.

All of heaven and Earth are within you.

To end this massage, heaven cups the receiver's head in his hands; Earth cups her ankles. Both gently pull their weight back away, stretching and elongating the body. Release. Repeat several times. Then just hold in stillness. Notice in the stillness, as receiver, with heaven and Earth holding you there, how you allow your body to elongate.

Ray of Light: Calling All Angels

Lucia is a client who always asks Erica to do an invocation before she starts a massage. She always asks for Jesus and Archangel Michael to be summoned to the session. After many a session, she will tell Erica that Michael gave her direction.

At the time, Lucia was working on changing the way she guarded herself. She was seeking to no longer guard herself out of fear but be protected by the "sword of truth," as she put it. She wanted to move from being fear-based to love-based. She was dealing with gaining more discernment between right and wrong. Highly critical of her self and sometimes of others, she wanted to allow the love to flow, to be more accepting and increase her compassion.

Touch was never very comfortable for Lucia, and it was hard for her to relax. Erica worked a lot in her neck and shoulders, rocking her legs out of her hips, just to open up places in her body. Lucia was very slim but had heavy legs. She was a very emotional person and not very grounded. It was as though her legs were heavier as a way of stabilizing herself.

Lucia was receptive to Archangel Michael because of her religious vocation, but she also was an angelic person, someone who was very caring and compassionate on a one-on-one level, though she could be smart and sassy outwardly. She was an altruistic person who was very pure-hearted, with a strong sense of right and wrong. She could not abide dishonesty. She could be passionate and very vocal when she sensed an injustice. She was working through massage to balance this, to soften her edges.

Lucia would tell Erica that archangel Michael transmitted assignments during sessions to do in the interim. For example, one was to create a shield for herself, decorating it with fabric. She placed the symbols of a rose and sword on it, signifying love and courage. Lucia continued working with Erica in massage sessions, summoning Archangel Michael and Jesus. Sometimes one would appear during a massage session, and Lucia would break to pray intently for 15 minutes. Then she would return to the massage table.

After this series of sessions, she married the man who was in her life. She moved to the West Coast to take a very powerful job. She returns to Erica from time to time, and Erica has noticed Lucia has more faith in herself and has softened her judgments about herself and others.

We shall find peace. We shall hear angels. We shall see the sky sparkling with diamonds.
—Anton Chekov, Russian writer

Signposts

Once you begin cultivating your experience of the wisdom in the collective unconscious during massage, you will find signposts along the way. Over time, these signposts will signal to you that you are approaching information that is truth, something you can trust. You may develop the sense of anticipation, of knowing when information is about to come. You may see your epiphanies coming.

When Erica was first playing with breath and movement, one of her teachers instructed her in moving a certain way, with her hands at her sides. Once during a movement session, Erica remembers stepping forward in a tai ch'i–like move, with her hands pushing forward. She felt and en-visioned violet and golden flames shoot out of her palms. It occurred to her in that moment that it was in that part of the palm where they ham-mered the nail into Jesus' hand. The synchronicity of that—connecting to Jesus' compassion and defenselessness—and the powerful vision of the experience became a signpost to her. When she is about to receive a psychic message, often she will start to see purple and gold, sometimes emerald green. It's a signal to her that she is opening, in the flow.

To begin attuning to your psychic signposts, start to notice the subtleties. Notice what resonates for you. Notice what clicks. Notice what sticks. We each have ways we are more naturally attuned to receive information and learn—a learning style. You may learn and remember something better if it's visual or verbal or aural. The ways are personal and indivi-dual, depending on your natural learning style, your religious background, your family upbringing. Some of us are more visual and may be attuned to colors. Others are more aural and may be attuned to vocal intonations.

Start now to attune to the subtle shifts that occur when someone speaking slips down into a deeper truth. Erica's experience of this is with a psychotherapist who would begin to speak with a slight clip, a subtle accent, when she approached a significant truth. Sometimes the shift is in language. Erica remembers in a Bill Moyers interview with teacher-mythologist Joseph Campbell when Campbell shifted from "I" to "we." At that shift, he was talking about a more universal truth, a higher knowledge.

You are getting near a deeper truth when your voice changes, when your eyesight shifts, when you move differently. You may talk more rapidly. Or you might slow down. Your movements might change, become quick and light. Carolyn remembers the day before her father died—a day in which he struggled to catch each breath—that her ears were stopped up. She was at work, unaware that his struggle had deepened. To her mind, her father was in the hospital an extra day because it was taking him a little longer to recuperate from back surgery. But her ears were psychically attuned to his struggle, as he began to cross over to death. Something in her knew. She commented to a co-worker that she couldn't hear, remarking that "I guess there's something I don't want to hear today." After his death, she continued to experience the connection to her father through her ears. A few days after his death, going to read his will, she experienced an inner ear disturbance, becoming dizzy and losing her balance. She became so overwhelmingly dizzy she had to stop the car to throw up.

These synchronicities in your body are your natural portals for psychic information. Now, Carolyn is attuned during massage sessions with Erica that her ears are a way in. When emotions that need to be released get stirred up, her ears get clogged. Because she recognizes it, she welcomes it and receives it. She breathes through it and waits for more information. Often the next message is from her father or another significant man in her life.

Start now in your next series of massage sessions to tune in to your portals. Does phlegm come up? Do your eyes get cloudy? Do your ears ring? Sometimes you will get referred pain. The massage therapist will be working with your feet and you feel it in the left kidney. Or it moves up the right side of the ribcage with a sizzle and pop, then shoots down the arm and out the fingertips. If you are attuned to these things, you can feel how things zip around inside you.

Erica once had a spiritual teacher advise that those on the other side cannot do it for us. They cannot hit us over the head to share their wisdom. All they can do is drop hints and clues. We have to tune in. We have to turn up the volume. Ask, watch, listen.

We are hoarding potentials so great that they are just about unimaginable.
—Jack Schwartz, human potential expert

In the metaphysical tradition, it is believed each of us comes into the physical world from the spiritual world on certain rays of light. People who ride in on a crimson ray have a certain job to do, while those who come in on purple or gold or indigo have another job to do. These rays are related to the frequencies of the different chakras. Each connects with a certain kind of intention.

Empowerment Exercise: Birth

Use this massage exercise to carry you back into a new world. Use it to tune yourself into the ray of light that brought you in, reactivating that ray's purpose and intention. Use it to welcome yourself back into a new, more meaningful life in which you continue to use the practice of massage from this book in your life. Think of it as a new birth of sorts.

Don't let the idea of auric fields shy you away from this exercise. Just experiment. Before starting, giver and receiver open to experiencing the colors of the energy flowing through their bodies and through the room. During the friction movements, you may begin to notice colors. When you are receiving and are on your back, with your partner holding her hands on your body, you may notice a different color. As the giver, as you step back through his energy field, what colors do you feel? Do they change?

Start with your partner on his tummy. Rub a small amount of oil into your hands. Cover his whole back with oil. Move so you are standing at his head. Knead through his neck and shoulder muscles, from the center out, pressing through the bumps and nodules with your fingers. Now place one flat hand on each side of his spine. Swoop down as far as you can to his buttocks. Use only light pressure because this is counter to heart flow. Think about how this movement is the opposite, about going back into the womb to be reborn. Move down to the bottom of the spine, then up the sides of the body back to the neck and shoulders. Do this several times.

Using the outer side of your hands (pinkie finger side), rub really fast down the back, on each side of the spine. Use a lot of back and forth movement, creating friction. You'll know you are doing it right if it gets very hot. When you reach the bottom of the spine, again do a sweep with the flat of your hands, up the sides, resting at the neck and shoulders.

Ask your partner to turn over on his back. Place your hands on his heart chakra and allegiance chakra. Rock gently. Rock until it feels like it should be still. Hold it. Allow your partner to deepen in the warmth of your hands.

Now step back from your partner, and see if you can do what is called stroking the outer levels of his aura. Start close, holding your open hands before you, as though you are touching the air around your partner's body. Hold it and gain a feel of his energy. Take a step back and feel the energy. Keep moving backward and see how far you go before you feel the outer edge of his energy.

To conclude this exercise, go to his feet. Place your hands on the soles of his feet. Say, "Welcome."

The Infinite

Massage can be a vehicle for the infinite. Massage puts us in the flow. It's about being here now, letting life force energy work through us. It's about connecting to something greater than ourselves that shows the meaning and purpose to our lives. It brings us to the dance, where we get to take the steps, make the choices. When you are doing massage, you become a conduit for all that is outside of what is seen or touched or felt or heard.

When we bring compassion, courage, and self-love to these exercises, we see their magic. When we bring intention to massage, we summon a great transformational power. When we come with openness to whatever the experience might bring, we invite ourselves to heal. When we keep practicing, bringing our time and energy to it, we can create this alchemic marriage between the need to know and the desire to transform. Massage allows us to have the revelation that brings about the transformation of body, mind, and spirit. Massage in its highest is that.

Resources

Books

Adamson, Eve, and Gary McClain, Ph.D. *Empowering Your Life with Joy.* Alpha Books, 2003.

Adamson, Eve, and Joan Budilovsky. *The Complete Idiot's Guide to Massage.* Alpha Books, 1998.

Anand, Margot. *The Art of Sexual Ecstasy: The Path of Sacred Sexuality for Western Lovers.* Jeremy P. Tarcher, 1989.

Barks, Coleman. *Essential Rumi.* HarperSanFrancisco, 1997.

Berkowitz, Rita, with Deborah S. Romaine. *Empowering Your Life with Angels.* Alpha Books, 2004.

Brennan, Barbara. *Hands of Light: A Guide to Healing Through the Human Energy Field.* Bantam, 1988.

Breuilly, Elizabeth, Joanne O'Brien, Martin E. Marty, and Martin Palmer. *Religions of the World: The Illustrated Guide to Origins, Beliefs, Traditions and Festivals.* Checkmark Books, 1997.

Britton, Patti, and Helen Hodgson. *The Complete Idiot's Guide to Sensual Massage.* Alpha Books, 2003.

Castaneda, Carlos. *Teaching Don Juan: A Yaqui Way of Knowledge.* Washington Square Press, 1985.

Eagle Feather, Ken. *The Toltec Way: A User's Guide to the Teachings of Don Juan Matus, Carlos Castaneda and Other Toltec Seers.* Hampton Road Publishing Co., 1995.

Feldman, Gail Carr, Ph.D., and Katherine A. Gleason. *Releasing the Goddess Within.* Alpha Books, 2003.

Flynn, Carolyn, and Arlene Tognetti. *The Intuitive Arts on Health.* Alpha Books, 2003.

Foundation of Inner Peace. *A Course in Miracles.* 1975.

Gibran, Kahlil. *The Prophet.* Knopf, 1923.

Gregg, Susan. *The Toltec Way: A Guide to Personal Transformation.* Renaissance Books, 2000.

Hanh, Thich Nhat. *Anger: Wisdom for Cooling the Flames.* Riverhead Books, 2002.

Honervogt, Tanmaya. *The Power of Reiki: An Ancient Hands-On Healing Technique.* Owl Books, 1998.

Iyengar, B.K.S., and Yehudi Manuhin. *Light on Pranayama: The Yogic Art of Breathing.* Crossroad/Herder and Herder, 1995.

Jenkinson, Ruth, Barbara Kunz, and Kevin Kunz. *Reflexology: Health at Your Fingertips.* DK Publishing, 2003.

Kern, Michael. *Wisdom in the Body: The Craniosacral Approach to Essential Health.* Thorsons Publishing, 2001.

Küstenmacher, Marion, and Werner Küstenmacher. *Mandalas for Power and Energy.* Sterling Publishing Co., 2003.

Lewis, C. S. *The Problem of Pain.* HarperSanFrancisco, 2001.

Lubeck, Walter. *The Spirit of Reiki: The Complete Handbook of the Reiki System.* Lotus Press, 2001.

Luby, Thia. *Children's Book of Yoga: Games and Exercises Mimic Plants and Animals and Objects.* Clear Light Publishing, 1998.

Lundberg, Paul. *The Book of Shiatsu: A Complete Guide to Using Hand Pressure and Gentle Manipulation to Improve Your Health, Vitality and Stamina.* Fireside, 2003.

Mares, Theun. *Cry of the Eagle.* Lionheart Publishing, 2002.

Meadows, Kenneth. *The Medicine Way: A Shamanic Path to Self-*

Mastery. Element Books Ltd., 1997.

Namikoshi, Toru. *The Complete Book of Shiatsu Therapy.* Japan Publications, 1994.

Ruiz, don Miguel. *The Four Agreements: A Practical Guide to Personal Freedom.* Amber-Allen Publishing, 1997.

———. *The Mastery of Love: A Practical Guide to the Art of Relationship, a Toltec Wisdom Book.* Amber-Allen Publishing, 1999.

Sills, Franklyn. *The Polarity Process: Energy as a Healing Art.* North Atlantic Books, 2002.

Stein, Diane. *Essential Reiki: A Complete Guide to an Ancient Healing Art.* Crossing Press, 1995.

Tolle, Eckhart. *The Power of Now: A Gateway to Spiritual Enlightenment.* New World Library, 1999.

———. *Stillness Speaks.* New World Library, 2003.

Toropov, Brandon, and Father Luke Buckles. *The Complete Idiot's Guide to World Religions, Second Edition.* Alpha Books, 2004.

Upledger, John, and Jon Vredevoogd. *Craniosacral Therapy.* Eastland Press, 1983.

Vigil, dona Bernadette. *Mastery of Awareness: Living the Four Agreements.* Inner Traditions International Ltd., 2001.

Wills, Pauline. *The Reflexology Manual: An Easy-to-Use Illustrated Guide to the Healing Zones of Hands and Feet.* Healing Arts Press, 1995.

Wolfe, Frankie Avalon, and Russel McAllister. *The Complete Idiot's Guide to Reflexology.* Alpha Books, 1999.

Websites

www.gracecathedral.org/labyrinth   Posts news about labyrinths around the world, guide to locating labyrinths. Part of the Grace Cathedral website, an Episcopal church in San Francisco.

www.labyrinthsociety.org   An organization for people who build, write about, and study labyrinths as a tool for transformation.

www.reflexology.com   A good resource for many reflexology sites on the web.

www.reflexology.org   A guide to reflexology organizations around the world.

www.theamt.com   The official site for the Association for Energy Meridian Therapies.

www.toltecwisdom.org   A site dedicated to practices of the Toltec way, in mastering awareness, transformation, and intent.

www.yogabasics.com   A comprehensive and user-friendly site that provides a full introduction to yoga.

Charts

Meridian charts can be found at massage schools, holistic health stores, or schools of traditional Chinese medicine. On the Internet, go to **www.theamt.com**. An online list of resources is at **www.watcheducation.com/acupuncture-chart.html**. An online interactive chart is available at **www.qi-journal.com/tcmarticles/acumodel.asp**.

Reflexology charts can be found at massage schools or holistic health stores. On the Internet, go to **www.reflexology.com, www.allheart.com, www.pressandrejuvenate.com, www.promedproducts.com,** or **anatomical.com**.

Index

The New Age Way
to Get What You Want Out of Life

Empowering Your Life with Wicca
ISBN: 0-02-864437-9
$14.95 US/$22.99 CAN

Empowering Your Life with Dreams
ISBN: 1-59257-092-5
$14.95 US/$22.99 CAN

Empowering Your Life with Joy
ISBN: 1-59257-097-6
$14.95 US/$22.99 CAN

Empowering Your Life with Runes
ISBN: 1-59257-165-4
$14.95 US/$22.99 CAN

Empowering Your Life with Yoga
ISBN: 1-59257-249-9
$14.95 US/$22.99 CAN

ISBN: 1-59257-241-3
$14.95 US/$22.99 CAN

ISBN: 1-59257-207-3
$14.95 US/$22.99 CAN

ISBN: 1-59257-268-5
$14.95 US/$22.99 CAN